*Penguin Critical Studies*

# Tennyson

Roger Ebbatson, who was born in Lincolnshire, is Senior Lecturer at Worcester College of Higher Education. He studied at the Universities of Sheffield and London and taught at colleges in London before moving to the University of Sokoto in Nigeria. He is the author of a number of articles on nineteenth-century and twentieth-century English literature and of two books, *Lawrence and the Nature Tradition* (1980) and *The Evolutionary Self: Hardy, Forster, Lawrence* (1983). He has also edited Thomas Hardy's *A Pair of Blue Eyes* and *The Trumpet-Major* for Penguin Classics.

*Penguin Critical Studies*
Joint Advisory Editors:
Stephen Coote and Bryan Loughrey

# *Tennyson*

**Roger Ebbatson**

Penguin Books

PENGUIN BOOKS

Published by the Penguin Group
27 Wrights Lane, London W8 5TZ, England
Viking Penguin Inc., 40 West 23rd Street, New York, New York 10010, USA
Penguin Books Australia Ltd, Ringwood, Victoria, Australia
Penguin Books Canada Ltd, 2801 John Street, Markham, Ontario, Canada L3R 1B4
Penguin Books (NZ) Ltd, 182–190 Wairau Road, Auckland 10, New Zealand

Penguin Books Ltd, Registered Offices: Harmondsworth, Middlesex, England

First published 1988

Made and printed in Great Britain by
Richard Clay Ltd, Bungay, Suffolk
Filmset in Monophoto Times

ENL(PC)
N64270X

In Memory:
E.M.E., H.W.E.

# Contents

# Introductory Note

I have tried in this book to provide a coherent short study of both context and text for the reader of Tennyson's poetry. The first part of the book examines biographical, ideological and stylistic questions, whilst the second part is given over to a detailed analysis of selected poems. In making a selection from Tennyson's large output I have sought to provide a commentary on those poems which remain most widely read and discussed, and have omitted consideration of *Idylls of the King* for reasons of space. My reading of Tennyson has been continuously stimulated by the widely divergent critical approaches of Christopher Ricks and Alan Sinfield, and my debts to both of them are registered in the text. I am most grateful to Catherine Neale for her help and advice. All quotations of the poetry are from *The Poems of Tennyson*, edited by Christopher Ricks (Longman, 1969).

R.E.

# Chronology

| | |
|---|---|
| 1809 | Born at Somersby, Lincolnshire. |
| 1816–20 | Attended Louth Grammar School. |
| 1827 | *Poems by Two Brothers* published at Louth. Entered Trinity College, Cambridge in November. |
| 1828 | Arthur Hallam entered Trinity College in October. |
| 1829 | Tennyson won the Chancellor's Gold Medal for his poem, 'Timbuctoo'. Joined the Apostles debating circle. Hallam visited Somersby at Christmas. |
| 1830 | Published *Poems, Chiefly Lyrical*. Undertook a journey to the Pyrenees with Hallam in support of a republican Spanish group. |
| 1831 | Dr Tennyson died. Tennyson left Cambridge. |
| 1832 | A tour of the Rhine with Hallam. *Poems* published in December. |
| 1833 | Hallam died in Vienna in September. |
| 1835 | Death of Tennyson's grandfather, the 'Old Man of the Wolds'. |
| 1836 | Tennyson fell in love with Emily Sellwood at the wedding of her sister to his brother Charles. This led on to a difficult and protracted courtship. |
| 1837 | The Tennyson family left Somersby for a house in Epping. |
| 1842 | *Poems* published in two volumes. |
| 1843 | The woodworking business in which Tennyson had invested most of his capital collapsed. The family moved to Cheltenham. |
| 1845 | Granted a Civil List pension. |
| 1847 | *The Princess* |
| 1850 | *In Memoriam* published. Tennyson and Emily Sellwood finally married, and Tennyson was offered the position of Poet Laureate after the death of Wordsworth. |
| 1851 | Tennyson and his wife began married life in Twickenham. |
| 1852 | Hallam Tennyson born. |
| 1853 | The family moved to Farringford on the Isle of Wight. Tennyson was later to become a valued friend of Queen Victoria and a frequent visitor to Osborne, her residence on the island. |
| 1854 | Birth of Lionel Tennyson. |
| 1855 | *Maud, and Other Poems*. |

1859    First group of *Idylls of the King* published.
1864    *Enoch Arden, and Other Poems.*
1865    Tennyson's mother died.
1868    Work began on Aldworth, the Tennysons' summer home in Surrey.
1870    *The Holy Grail and Other Poems.*
1872    *Gareth and Lynette, etc.*
1879    Tennyson's favourite brother Charles died.
1880    *Ballads and Other Poems.*
1884    Tennyson took his seat in the House of Lords. *Becket.*
1885    *Tiresias and Other Poems.*
1886    *Locksley Hall Sixty Years After.*
1889    *Demeter and Other Poems.*
1892    Died 6 October at Aldworth. Buried in Westminster Abbey.

# 1. The Life of Tennyson

The Tennysons first settled in the East Riding of Yorkshire. In the eighteenth century Michael Tennyson, an apothecary, married the heiress of the wealthy Clayton family which owned a large part of Grimsby in Lincolnshire. The Claytons claimed descent from the holders of the d'Eyncourt baronetcy. Michael's son George set up as a solicitor at Market Rasen in north Lincolnshire and married Mary Turner from nearby Caistor. George was an astute businessman, though hot-headed by nature. He became owner of the manor estate of Beacons, the d'Eyn-court property, near the village of Tealby. He improved this estate and renamed it Bayons Manor. He had two sons, but decided at an early age that the elder, George Clayton Tennyson, should be passed over in favour of the younger, Charles. From this decision many of the troubles which afflicted the poet's family were to stem. George Clayton, a sensitive but difficult man who probably suffered from epilepsy, went to St John's College, Cambridge, and was ordained as deacon in 1801. After a possibly mythical journey to Russia, he was ordained as priest in 1802. He married Elizabeth Fytche of Louth in 1805, and in 1806 was awarded the livings of Bag Enderby and Somersby near Horncastle, where the family were to live until his death, thirty years later. George's elder sister, Elizabeth, married a great Durham coal-owner, Major Matthew Russell, who bought and 'medievalized' Brancepeth Castle with the aid of Charles Tennyson, whom Russell got into Parliament. George Clayton Tennyson and his family entered Somersby Rectory in 1808, and ten of the twelve children were born there.

Life in a small hamlet in the Lincolnshire Wolds meant that the family had to fall back upon their own resources. Dr Tennyson played the harp, wrote verse and read voraciously. Mrs Tennyson was a pious Evangelical, but noted for her good humour. The Tennysons were not poor, but suffered under the preferential treatment which the elder George, the 'Old Man of the Wolds', gave to Charles and his family. Alfred and his two older brothers attended Louth Grammar School. The landscape of the Wolds, and the flat marshlands stretching away to the sea, began to haunt Tennyson, as did certain conjunctions of sound, such as 'far, far away', which he would recite endlessly.

He had begun to compose verse at the age of eight, and in 1824 grief at the death of his favourite poet led him to engrave 'Byron is dead' in sandstone near the local brook. Problems multiplied at the Rectory: Dr Tennyson suffered increasingly from attacks of epilepsy and depression, and several of the sons showed signs of instability. These temperamental problems, allied to the grievance over the inheritance, were the roots of that 'black blood' of the Tennysons to which the poet referred with glum satisfaction. Nevertheless, the boys enjoyed the environment of the Wolds, and their love of Malory's *Morte d'Arthur* enabled them to hold mock jousting tournaments in the woods. Tennyson, who was specially close to his brothers Charles and Frederick, also loved the family holidays at Mablethorpe and elsewhere on the coast.

As Dr Tennyson's health declined he took refuge in drink and (like his son Charles) in opium. The Tennyson brothers published in Louth in 1827 *Poems by Two Brothers*, the two being Alfred and Charles, though Frederick also contributed to this volume. In this year Alfred and Charles joined Frederick at Trinity College, Cambridge. They were an oddly dressed and striking-looking group, notably Alfred, who was tall and powerfully built, with dark, aquiline features. After violent ructions at the Rectory, Mrs Tennyson and the younger children left home, and Dr Tennyson then agreed to seek treatment in Paris. Although these problems clouded Alfred's time at Cambridge, his life changed significantly in his second year, when he met Arthur Hallam. The son of a leading historian, and close friend of the young Gladstone, Hallam was widely regarded as a man of outstanding powers. He was an eloquent debater, and fervent lover of Italian art and thought. With Alfred, in 1829 Hallam joined the Apostles, an elite debating society at Cambridge, and in the same year the poet was awarded the Chancellor's Medal for his poem, 'Timbuctoo'. Alfred published his *Poems, Chiefly Lyrical* in 1830, the same year as his brother Charles successfully published his *Sonnets*.

Hallam had first visited Somersby at Christmas 1829, and soon fell in love with Emily Tennyson. They became engaged, though Mr Hallam did not fully approve the match. Dr Tennyson returned to the Rectory in 1830, and in the same year Alfred and Arthur Hallam made an expedition to Spain. They were involved in an attempt by English intellectuals to help finance an insurrection of exiled liberal forces against the throne of Ferdinand VII. Their role was to carry money and messages to the Pyrenees. The attempt was to end in disaster with the deaths of the rebel leader, General Torrijos, and of one of the Apostles, Robert Boyd. The Apostles grossly misjudged the situation, misled by their idealistic naivety in a complex political situation. Despite the fiasco, Tennyson was to recall the impact of the landscape, notably the valley of Cauteretz, in subsequent poems.

Dr Tennyson, after many years of suffering and upheaval, died in March 1831. In the summer of the following year Tennyson visited the Rhineland with Arthur Hallam, who was now reluctantly studying the law. Tennyson's 1832 volume of poems received largely favourable notices, but the poet was deeply wounded by a vituperative review by J. W. Croker in the *Quarterly Review*, and this led to the ten-year gap in publication which then ensued. In the middle of 1833 Hallam went on a European tour with his father; he was taken ill in Vienna and died of apoplexy on 15 September. The ship containing his body returned to England at the end of the year, and he was buried in January 1834 at Clevedon, near the Bristol Channel. Tennyson began to compose some of the lyrics about Hallam's death which would finally become *In Memoriam*. Although desolated, he did make other friendships at this time, notably with Edward Fitzgerald who was to be the 'translator' of *The Rubaiyat of Omar Khayyam*. About this time the Old Man of the Wolds persuaded his favoured son Charles to eschew his parliamentary ambitions and return to the estates in Lincolnshire. Tennyson's elder brother Charles, who was battling with opium addiction, came into money and inherited the living of Grasby, where he was to live for the rest of his life as a sonneteering parson. In 1836 Charles, who adopted the surname Turner, married Louisa Sellwood, the daughter of a Horncastle solicitor. Tennyson, who seems to have earlier admired various young women, including the socially elevated Rosa Baring of Harrington Hall, with whom he had an unhappy relationship, now fell in love with Louisa's sister Emily. The courtship was to be hesitant and protracted over the next fourteen years.

The Old Man of the Wolds died in 1835, leaving the bulk of his fortune to his son Charles, who now set about rebuilding Bayons Manor in a grandiose 'medieval' style. For the next ten years or more, Tennyson led a highly unsettled existence. He had to organize the removal of the family from Somersby to Epping in June 1837, and began to lead a somewhat wandering life, as he disliked suburbia. Because of his lack of prospects, Mr Sellwood ordered that Tennyson and Emily should stop meeting. At the instigation of some of the Apostles Tennyson agreed to revise some of his extant poems and produce several new ones, and this led to the successful two-volume *Poems* of 1842 which contained much of his most characteristic work. He invested £3000 in a woodworking business run by Dr Allen of the High Beech mental home near Epping. The venture failed in 1843, and Allen died in 1845. 'What with ruin in the distance and hypochondriacs in the foreground I feel very crazy,' Tennyson remarked, and the family situation must indeed have given him pause for thought: Frederick was wandering aimlessly in Italy, Charles wrestling with his opium addiction, Edward permanently consigned to a lunatic asylum at York, and Septimus being treated at High Beech for instability. Nevertheless, the poet's own position improved somewhat with the award of a Civil List pension of £200 per annum, and he was beginning to meet many of the luminaries of the day, such as Wordsworth, Thackeray, Dickens and Browning. He himself was several times treated for nervous depression, and tried the water cure at Malvern on a number of occasions. He remained in touch with Emily Sellwood, but she was frequently worried by his free-thinking tendencies. His elegies about Hallam began to be privately circulated, and pleased Emily by their religious feeling. In 1850, his *annus mirabilis*, Tennyson finally published *In Memoriam* and married Emily Sellwood. The death of Wordsworth in the same year paved the way for his acceptance of the post of Poet Laureate.

The remainder of Tennyson's life was far more stable, as his popularity increased and he became widely regarded as the poetic voice of his age. After living for a time in Twickenham, he and his family moved to a large mansion called Farringford on the Isle of Wight in 1853, initially leasing and eventually buying the property. Their first son, Hallam, was born in 1852, and the second, Lionel, in 1854, the year in which 'The Charge of the Light Brigade' proved very popular with the British public. He published *Maud* in 1855, the same year in which he received a doctorate from the University of Oxford. Emily was a semi-invalid and the Tennysons lived a secluded life on the island, though one which was increasingly prey to sightseers and admiring visitors, whom Tennyson dreaded. The Poet Laureate was a favourite of the Queen, whom he frequently visited at Osborne, her house on the island. He worked steadily at the *Idylls of the King*, the first group of which were published in 1859, and also began to experiment with Lincolnshire dialect poems. His mother died in 1865, and three years later the Tennysons commissioned a fancifully 'Gothic' mansion called Aldworth from their friend James Knowles. This was situated in Surrey, and was utilized as a summer residence. Tennyson had developed an interest in the theatre, and began to compose historical verse dramas such as *Queen May*, *Harold*, *Becket* and *The Foresters*, based upon Robin Hood. In 1879 Tennyson's favourite brother Charles died, and his collected sonnets were published the following year. At his friend Gladstone's behest, Tennyson entered the House of Lords in 1884; Hallam Tennyson married the same year, but continued to act as his father's amanuensis. In 1886 Lionel caught a fever and died on the way home from India. Tennyson himself died on 6 October 1892 at Aldworth, and was buried in Westminster Abbey with great ceremony, though the Queen did not attend. Emily Tennyson died in 1896, and a year later Hallam Tennyson published his compendious memoir of his father.

## 2. Tennyson, Hallam and their Age

The failure of their Spanish adventure seems to have coincided with a deepening sense of dissatisfaction among the Cambridge Apostles. In Britain the years preceding the Reform Bill were marked by factionalism, political upheaval and variously inspired outbreaks of violence. Hallam wrote to one of the group at the end of 1830, 'The country is in a more awful state than you can well conceive. The laws are almost suspended; the money of foreign factions is at work with a population exasperated into reckless fury.' 'Captain Swing', the legendary leader of the rick-burners in the south of England, had appeared in Cambridgeshire. Many students, including some Apostles, turned out to fight fires in the surrounding country. According to a poem of the period, the student body were confronted by 'starving, stalwart men, marching on the town', and they accordingly prepared themselves for battle. Nevertheless, the attitude of the Apostles was certainly not one of simple repression; there was, on the contrary, sympathy for the labouring class and perplexity in solving the problems of the time. The Apostles often looked to their spiritual guide, F. D. Maurice, for wisdom, and they shared his sense of horror at factionalism. This horror did not, however, lead the Apostles into the quiet retreats of aestheticism, and many recalled Trench's admonition of the poet, 'Tennyson, we cannot live in art'. The Apostles generally were suspicious of the new Reform Bill and felt that civil war was now a real possibility.

Whilst some Apostles sought refuge in the Evangelical Christian Socialism espoused by Maurice, this path was temperamentally un-congenial to Tennyson. He and Hallam were the focus within the group for the belief that a new age of literature was at hand after the early deaths of the major Romantic poets. Tennyson was never a leading spirit within the Apostles, saying little at their meetings and preferring to smoke his ubiquitous pipe; but despite the charismatic authority wielded by Hallam, most agreed that it was Tennyson who would be the poetic spokesman of the future. For a body of men who prided themselves upon their self-conscious rebellion against the literary values of the old guard, Tennyson's appearance was literally and metaphorically a god-send. The faith of the Apostles in modern poetry and in a Coleridgean metaphysic of the imagination was central to Hallam, who frequently explored the directions of the new poetry in a society so divided against itself. Hallam, whose family roots were in the West Country, disliked much about Cambridge, 'this college-studded marsh', as he termed it, and his philosophical papers were partly a response to personal unhappiness at this time. His review of Tennyson's *Poems, Chiefly Lyrical* in the *Englishman's Magazine* for August 1831 is a significant attempt to elevate an aesthetic theory of poetry above contemporary party battles. Nevertheless the Apostles' general tendency was to urge Tennyson towards a deep sense of duty to his age, and in his 1832 volume he injudiciously claimed, 'Mine be the power which ever for its sway/ Will win the wise at once, and by degrees/ May into uncongenial spirits flow'. Such statements provoked a devastating review by John Croker, and a ten-year gap before the poet would be tempted to publish again. The poetry of this period does indeed articulate the clash in ideology between an aesthetic stance as argued by Hallam, and the more socially responsible stress of the Apostles generally.

In Hallam's view, opinion and belief were central to the human condition, and problems of belief focused most acutely upon religious questions. In his paper for the society, 'On Sympathy', Hallam traced the origins of sympathetic feeling to infantile experience and demonstrated its role in developing a moral sense in the individual. A later essay would suggest that human love finds its real fulfilment through religious faith. Love, Hallam argues here, in its ethical role is a desire for 'another's gratification, and consequent aversion to another's pain'. Proper attention to the world of the senses can be connected to a spiritual reality so as to effect 'a regeneration of the soul' in the individual. Morality exists, Hallam urges, 'under the aspect of beauty', and he follows Plato in praising homosexual love as the 'highest and purest manly love'. The efforts of the intellect are 'posterior to the work of feeling', and it is God alone who understands the 'abysmal secrets of personality'. Hallam died too young to formulate a consistent position, but he may be observed here grappling to reconcile aestheticism and faith in a manner directly relevant to the poetry of his friend. As Tennyson recalled in *In Memoriam*, the effect of Hallam's eloquent persuasion was hypnotic:

> . . . A willing ear
> We lent him. Who, but hung to hear
> The rapt oration flowing free

(87)

There was much in the concerns of the Apostles which harked back to Romanticism, a movement in which the problematic question of the

7

relation of consciousness to nature is fundamental. Wordsworth's account of the organic links of sympathy between mind and nature, Coleridge's insistence upon the seminal role of the imagination, and Keats's sense of the intensity and negativity of poetic identity were all characteristic of the movement. The Romantic poets emphasize self-realization to a revolutionary degree; whilst Tennyson follows them, there is a greater feeling of passivity in his poems, in which states of feeling are luxuriantly indulged for their own sake. The early poetry especially tends towards morbidity of feeling, that sense of the mind's alienation from the outer world which had already marked Coleridge's 'Dejection Ode' and partially clouded Wordsworth's 'Resolution and Independence'. The dominant terms of Tennyson's reaction to self and age might better be described as irresolution and dependence. Through much of the early work, what a poem by Philip Larkin was to term 'desire for oblivion' runs counter to the stated theme; there is what Tennyson called a 'loss of personality' which seemed 'not extinction but the only true life'. This loss harks back to some of the central visionary moments of Romantic poetry in Wordsworth's *The Prelude* or *Tintern Abbey*, for instance, where the loss is ultimately found to be a gain.

The deep polarity in the debates of the Apostles corresponded to such a dilemma in Tennyson's mind, a polarization between demands of responsibility and sensibility. The high poetic gifts which Wordsworth, in the preface to *Lyrical Ballads*, had claimed as giving the poet 'a more comprehensive soul', become in Tennyson a means of separating the poet from man and society. This separation was to fire some of the poet's most successful works, such as 'The Lady of Shalott' and 'The Lotos-Eaters'. In a commercial age seemingly unpropitious to poetry, the role of poet was subject to pressure and dislocation to a high degree. The effortful sense of the poetic mind travailing to reconcile itself with society would, according to Hallam, account for the melancholy which he detected as 'the spirit of modern poetry'. Thus was Tennyson increasingly aware in the early thirties of his role, and of others' expectations for him in relation to his society. In a poem like 'Oenone', in the 1832 volume, he explored the possibility of reconciling feelings and morality. At the centre of the story of the judgement of Paris lies a choice between worldly power offered by Juno, philosophical wisdom offered by Pallas, and sensual love offered by Venus. In this work and elsewhere we may detect signs of Tennyson facing up to the narcissism in his own makeup, but the overall effect of the poem remains confusing for the reader. 'The Palace of Art' rehearses the argument more clearly, and was written in direct response to the admonition of Tennyson's fellow Apostle, R. C. Trench: 'We cannot live in art'. The central image of the poem is that of the Soul dwelling in her pleasure-palace. The work begins with a description of the ornate palace itself, then moves on to a catalogue of tapestries of landscapes which represent different moods, then a series of reflections upon various myths and legends, followed by portraits of great artists and poets.

The Soul gains a progressive awareness of her own powers, and gradually the mind is subjected to the probing inquiry of God, an analysis which is imaged in a phrase borrowed from Hallam:

> The abysmal deeps of Personality,
> Plagued her with sore despair.

The Soul decides to leave the palace and engage with the world, but this resolution is undermined by the vividness of the vocabulary of gloom, as in this almost subliminal evocation of the Lincolnshire coastline:

> One seem'd all dark and red – a tract of sand,
>   And some one pacing there alone,
> Who paced for ever in a glimmering land,
>   Lit with a low large moon.

To speak of such an art in relation to a statically conceived set of 'Victorian values' is misleading and misconceived. Although it was outwardly marked by peace and increasing prosperity, intellectual and social ferment is rife in the documents of the age. Whilst much of Tennyson's work indirectly both reflects and creates this ferment, in certain texts he did seek to address social questions explicitly, though never unequivocally. As the son of a Lincolnshire parson the poet's sympathies lay instinctively with the conservative rural class, but it was a sympathy undermined by the effects of his family's disinherited state. The emotions aroused by the aggrandizement of the 'd'Eyncourt' Tennysons perhaps led the poet to speak for progress and gradual change within a paradoxically conservative mode. There is, pervasively in Tennyson, a looking back to an idealized past, often medieval, which is partly temperamental and partly due to the overpowering influence within the early Victorian period of Thomas Carlyle. Under the pressure of the rick-burnings he had witnessed near Cambridge, and the more widespread revolutionary movements throughout Europe at this time, Tennyson wrote a number of poems which advocated adherence to a constitutional form of government. In his aphoristic poem, 'Of Old sat Freedom on the Heights', for instance, Tennyson ducks the issue of the revolution to extol a vaguely conceived and static 'Freedom' which seems little related to the contemporaneous agricultural riots and the culminating transportation of the Tolpuddle Martyrs in 1834. The Reform Bill of 1832 was designed to head off trouble not by offering the vote to the working people but by bringing manufacturing and commercial interests into Parliament. Tennyson saw this Bill as a necessary antidote to subversion and worse:

> What nobler than an ancient land
> That passing an august decree
> Makes wider in a settled peace
> The lists of liberty?
>
> What baser than a land that falls
> From freedom crying on her name
> Through cycles of disastrous change
> To forge the links of shame?
>
> ('I loving Freedom for herself')

The high valuation of freedom here sits uneasily with the suspicion that such a freedom will be endangered by the joining together of the unenfranchised working classes – Dickens was to rehearse such arguments later in *Hard Times.* Whatever reservations the shiftless and melancholic poet may have felt about the Carlylean doctrine of the saving efficacy of work, he shared the sage's quasi-feudal vision of a land in which different classes work together in unity under strong but moderate leadership. Like Dickens, George Eliot, Kingsley and Mrs Gaskell in the novel, Tennyson feels uneasy about the blighting effects of unfettered industrial expansion and *laissez-faire* capitalism; and like them, his solutions laid stress upon changes in personal feeling between the classes. His idealizing tendency finds expression in poems which expound commitment to freedom whilst retaining the overall class structure of the modern state. In one of the most interesting of these early political poems, 'You ask me, why, tho' ill at ease', Tennyson seems almost able to interrogate the contradictions of his own position. Freedom, the poem argues, is not to remain seated distantly on the heights above; it becomes appropriately Victorian, 'sober-suited', and thus 'slowly broadens down' through the years. Yet the poet feels 'ill at ease' at this bourgeois prospect, and longs 'for the purple seas'. As often with Tennyson, the poem reveals in its subtext a desire for escape, a nostalgia for a return to an oceanic maternal womb whence contradiction and stress are banished:

> Tho' Power should make from land to land
>   The name of Britain trebly great –
>   Tho' every channel of the State
> Should fill and choke with golden sand –
>
> Yet waft me from the harbour-mouth,
>   Wild wind! I seek a warmer sky,
>   And I will see before I die
> The palms and temples of the South.

In another of the 1833 poems, 'Hail Briton!', Tennyson elaborates upon the nature of Britishness, and adverts to what he would call, in *In Memoriam*, 'the blind hysterics of the Celt'. Here national pride and fear of the alien are curiously conjoined. The excluded 'Other' exerts a strong pull on the imagination of the hegemonic group:

> Yet fear that passion may convulse
> Thy judgement: fear the neighbourhood
> Of that unstable Celtic blood
> That never keeps an equal pulse.

The poem expresses an apprehension that 'love of novel forms' will 'avail To quench the light of Reverence', a light which also shines strongly in 'Love thou thy land':

> But pamper not a hasty time,
>   Nor feed with crude imaginings
>   The herd, wild hearts and feeble wings
> That every sophister can lime.

The complex of feelings welling up in Tennyson about national issues is more extensively explored in later poems, such as the occasional poem, 'Ode on the Death of the Duke of Wellington' of 1852. The poet's uneasy ambivalence vis-à-vis the class system, his sympathy for the labouring class united to his deep distaste for wider democratization, threw up many sharp contradictions. Such uneasiness is often displayed in the formal properties of the work, notably in Tennyson's pervasive tendency to distance himself from his speakers: the central male figure in *The Princess* is subject to recurrent fainting fits; the 'Supposed Confessions' are those 'of a second-rate sensitive mind'; the hero of *Maud* is verging on insanity. Tennyson lived uncomfortably in an unheroic age, his brand of Christianized humanism at odds with much that he saw around him. This lack of sympathy is often dramatically revealed, as in 'Locksley Hall', or even more extensively in *Maud*. The vacillation and uncertainty dramatized in such poems is the source of much of the poet's best work, but it goes hand in hand with a desire, almost hysterical at times, for certainty and stability. Equilibrium is only really discovered in moments of private feeling and recollection, as in this finely crafted memory, thirty years after the event, of his visit to the Pyrenees with Hallam:

> All along the valley, while I walk'd today,
> The two and thirty years were a mist that rolls away;
> For all along the valley, down thy rocky bed,
> Thy living voice to me was as the voice of the dead,
> And all along the valley, by rock and cave and tree,
> The voice of the dead was a living voice to me.
>
> ('In the Valley of Cauteretz')

This characteristic warmth of response is significantly muffled in one of Tennyson's most popular poems of the same period, 'Enoch Arden', where the action turns upon a sailor's lengthy absence and a case of unintentional bigamy. The text here contrives to side-step the crucial issue which it raises relating to class structure, sexuality and Victorian litigation, in order to set up a life of self-denial and abstinence as a good in itself. The body of ideas lurking behind this and other of Tennyson's experiments in narrative form relate to the middle-class Victorian vision of woman as 'the angel in the house', a vision readily consumed by his readership. The idealization and exaltation of woman, and the worship of domesticity as her sacred role, served to conceal some of the sexual contradictions of a society where prostitution and sexual exploitation were rife. A work like 'Enoch Arden' might profitably be juxtaposed with a study like Steven Marcus's *The Other Victorians* for its complicity in such idealization to be fully registered. In *The Princess* (1847) Tennyson had interestingly addressed the issues of female liberation and education. The reader today is likely to be put off by the artificiality of the poem, based as it is on a tale-telling contest between a number of young men who simultaneously worship and denigrate women. The seven students each tell a story prompted by Lilia's espousal at Vivian Place of women's cause. Lilia expresses the wish that she were a princess, able to build 'Far off from men a college like a man's', where she would teach 'all that men are taught'. In between the stories the women characteristically are called upon to bring light relief in the form of a song – the magnificent series of lyrics embedded within the framing narrative. At the end the 'princess' is compelled to acknowledge that her programme for change will never be achieved, and that she will devote herself to child-bearing. Nevertheless, Tennyson does manage, within this absurd and constricting structure with all its manifest contradictions, to convey a sense of women as somehow acting as life-giving centres of civilization. There is a questioning, in the text, of the received views of womanhood, even if those views are finally endorsed, and it is a questioning which seems, in Tennyson's mind, inextricably linked with the Victorian preoccupation with matters of gentlemanliness.

An underlying problem which dogs Tennyson's poems the more potently for remaining unstated is the troublesome and anomalous position of the poet in an age of steam. In the prevailing utilitarian atmosphere engendered by Mill and Bentham (and satirically distorted in Dickens's *Hard Times*) the validity and purpose of imaginative literature were increasingly questioned. It seemed to many observers that science was replacing literature, and one characteristic defence was to urge that imaginative writing sought to explore states of mind rather than the world of 'reality'. In this view, there was a role for the poet even in an unquestionably materialistic age. This ideal of the poet as a kind of high priest of sensation and feeling, urged by Hallam in his famous review of Tennyson, was to lead to the increasing polarization evident in the place of writing towards the end of the century, with the rise of the so-called 'decadents' and the doctrine 'art for art's sake'. Tennyson always sought to retain a central position within his society, but there was much within him and in the very act of writing that was forcing him towards the margins. Such early poems as 'The Palace of Art' and 'The Lady of Shalott' circle warily around the problem that was to pose itself at every stage of his long career.

T. S. Eliot suggested that Tennyson was 'the most instinctive rebel against the society in which he was the most perfect conformist', and such ambivalence is neatly registered in his main work as laureate, the *Idylls of the King*. This long series of Arthurian tales, composed over many years, is framed by a panegyric to Albert and Victoria which led Swinburne to dub the last poem 'Morte d'Albert'. Whilst the framing verse is written in a standardly patriotic mode which Tennyson could always command at will, the narrative episodes themselves describe the rise and fall of a nation, and the emphasis is heavily upon decline. Camelot is a visionary city undermined by sin and infidelity. The *Idylls* had begun life long before the 1860s in 1833 with the composition of 'Morte d'Arthur', a striking and powerful work taking as its unspoken motivation the death of Arthur Hallam, and the consequent temporary dissolution of the Cambridge Apostles. The *Idylls* thus proceed from a different premise and move in a different direction from *In Memoriam*:

Arthur's failure seems to be that of the spiritual part of mankind to conquer its sensual drives. The failure of idealism is dramatized variously in the madness of Pelleas, the fratricide of Balan and Balin, the cynicism of Tristram, and the almost *fin de siècle* disillusionment of Merlin:

> Then fell on Merlin a great melancholy;
> He walk'd with dreams and darkness, and he found
> A doom that ever poised itself to fall,
> An ever-moaning battle in the mist,
> World-war of dying flesh against the life,
> Death in all life and lying in all love,
> The meanest having power upon the highest,
> And the high purpose broken by the worm.
>
> ('Merlin and Vivien')

Merlin's despair often resounds through the poetry of Tennyson, negating that belief in progress and upward development which is so widely insisted upon in the verse. So often are the positives and certainties of the Victorian age undermined in Tennyson's verse that it becomes a pervasive mark of his fictional heroes. The narrator of 'Locksley Hall', for instance, is an upper-class gentleman who feels unsuited to the Gradgrind world he inhabits, and the poem explores the contradictory urges he feels towards participation and escape. The villain in the tale is the commercial energy and competition which 'gilds the straitened forehead of the fool' and robs the narrator of his sweetheart. At the same time, the poem acknowledges the ambiguous desirability of 'progress':

> For I dipt into the future, far as human eye could see,
> Saw the Vision of the world, and all the wonder that would be;
>
> Saw the heavens fill with commerce, argosies of magic sails,
> Pilots of the purple twilight, dropping down with costly bales;

This high-minded evolution of commercialism leads inexorably towards the triumph of democracy and 'the Parliament of man, the Federation of the world', a vision which is precariously balanced with the sense of the revolutionary potential in current social inequality: 'Slowly comes a hungry people, as a lion creeping nigher'. Such a premonition of social crisis mingles awkwardly with the theme of blighted love to lead the hero towards the daydream of 'Summer isles of Eden lying in dark-purple spheres of sea', or the extraordinary regression into barbarism towards the end of the poem. The hero sees progress as a movement away from such barbarity, but is transfixed with anger at the rampant commercialism which has robbed him of his beloved Amy.

'Locksley Hall' derives much of its undoubted interest from that irreconcilable conjunction of civilization with repression which Freud was to explore. At the end the hero will, we are assured, follow 'the mighty wind' to the sea, whilst Locksley Hall and all it stands for within the social context will be destroyed in the storm that is coming. In the sequel, 'Locksley Hall Sixty Years After', the narrator speaks bitterly of the emptiness of the Whig doctrine of progress to which he had adhered as a young man:

> Gone the cry of 'Forward, Forward,' lost within a growing gloom;
> Lost, or only heard in silence from the silence of a tomb.

The issue here, and in other social and political poems, is for the poet to conceive how mankind can move down the 'ringing grooves of change' without revolution or recourse to authoritarian power.

In his relation to the external world of nature Tennyson similarly embodies discrepant attitudes and tensions. To over-simplify, there is an uneasy conjunction in his poems between the attitude to nature exemplified in the Romantic movement and the new scientific determinism of his own period. Often Tennyson, who was notoriously short-sighted, surprises and delights the reader with his uncanny closeness and accuracy of detailed vision, as in the sight of the girl's hair in 'The Brook':

> ... her hair
> In gloss and hue the chestnut, when the shell
> Divides threefold to show the fruit within.

With more complexity, Tennyson often endows a landscape with an emotional charge which relates very inwardly to a complex of feelings about the age, as when the narrator of *Maud* views the 'dreadful hollow' in terms of his own morbidity.

Many of the spiritual and emotional problems which were exercising his contemporaries weave themselves into the fabric of Tennyson's verse. One of the most significant documents in this respect is the 'Supposed Confessions of a Second-Rate Sensitive Mind' of 1830, which was already worrying away at some of the issues to be dramatized in *Maud*. The speaker has searched for the truth by practising a questioning attitude to life:

> Shall we not look into the laws
> Of life and death, and things that seem,
> And things that be, and analyse
> Our double nature, and compare
> All creeds till we have found the one,
> If one there be?

15

The speaker has lost his Christian faith, a matter for regret here, but this faith returns in a slightly later poem, 'The Two Voices', begun in 1833, where rhyming tetrameters create an aphoristic mode of utterance at odds with the heuristic tentativeness of much of Tennyson's ruminative verse. A sense of resonant doubt illumines a much finer poem like 'Ulysses'. The underlying sense of this monologue, according to the poet, is 'a sense of loss and all that had gone by', balanced by the thought that 'still life must be fought out to the end'.

The dialectic of loss and faith is of course most centrally explored in *In Memoriam*, where the mood changes from stark and dramatic grief, through reminiscence and neurotic collapse, towards an assertion of renewed faith. As an epilogue to the poem Tennyson added a section celebrating the marriage of one of his sisters and predicting the 'crowning race' of the future:

> Whereof the man, that with me trod
>   This planet, was a noble type
>   Appearing ere the times were ripe,
> That friend of mine who lives in God,
>
> That God, which ever lives and loves,
>   One God, one law, one element,
>   And one far-off divine event,
> To which the whole creation moves.

(Epilogue)

Whilst *In Memoriam* expresses the age's questions about faith, it is also a personal poem which reflects upon death, survival after death, and the existence of a deity. As for many Christians, the problem of evil is a difficult one here, and the poet is constrained to hope 'that somehow good/ Will be the final goal of ill'. If God is benevolent, how can nature be so careless of the individual? All Tennyson can bring himself to do is 'faintly trust the larger hope'.

Even the view that nature takes care of the 'type' is questioned: a 'thousand types' have irrevocably disappeared. Geology shows how many species have perished, and the materialist reading of life proposed by science corrodes the poet's faith as it was to threaten the belief of so many Victorian thinkers. Is man himself, the poem asks, destined to 'Be blown about the desert dust,/ Or sealed within the iron hills?' (56)

The ardent Darwinian, T. H. Huxley, claimed that 'Tennyson was the first poet since Lucretius who understood the drift of science.' Certainly, when the popularizing *Vestiges of Creation* by Robert Chambers appeared in 1844, the poet had for some years been familiar with its main line of argument. Indeed, quasi-evolutionary notions had already been inscribed in the middle sections of *In Memoriam*, composed in the 1830s. Yeats was to complain that 'brooding over scientific opinion ... extinguishes the central flame in Tennyson', but such meditation is more often a site for fruitful poetic creation. Lyell's *Principles of Geology* (1830–33) provided a crucial source for Tennyson's visionary apprehension of life as the product of physical forces. In section 118 of *In Memoriam* the issue of geological change is close to the heart of the argument. The poet first sees the earth emerging in 'tracts of fluent heat', an emergence followed by cataclysmic change, 'cyclic storms' which lead to a succession of species culminating in man, 'The herald of a higher race'. Such notions bear an ethical construction, since the poet advises the reader to expel 'the beast' within.

For Tennyson, belief in a deity seems to entail a logical belief in eternal life: 'We cannot give up the mighty hopes that make us men,' he remarks. The theology of *In Memoriam* falls far short of a full Christian faith and commitment, but its dramatization of the flux and change of 'honest doubt' remains at the roots of the poet's persona for the rest of his career. In 'The Holy Grail' (1869), for instance, the gradual dissolution of the Round Table is ascribed to the obsessive quest for mystical experience. Arthur ruminates upon the notion that a man should 'not wander from the allotted field/ Before his work is done'. But the king goes on to describe the nature of visionary moments in revelatory terms, speaking of:

> ... moments when he feels he cannot die,
> And knows himself no vision to himself,
> Nor the high God a vision, nor that One,
> Who rose again:

And in one of Tennyson's favourite poems of his later years, 'The Ancient Sage' (1885), the poet tells how, when he repeats his own name:

> The mortal limit of the Self was loosed,
> And past into the Nameless, as a cloud
> Melts into Heaven.

Such trance-like moments, to which the poet apparently had access from boyhood onwards, seem to emphasize the threadbare nature of materialism in the nineteenth century. That materialism is nowhere more pessimistically interrogated than in another late poem, 'Vastness' (1885). Here Tennyson reviews a world dominated by 'raving politics' and

17

'national hatreds', confused by the rival claims of competing philosophies and religions. It seems possible for the poet to conceive, in this mood, that 'we all of us end but in being our own corpse-coffins at last', and the poem adumbrates what Hardy, in *Jude the Obscure*, would call the 'coming universal wish not to live' – an immense death-wish which would culminate in the Great War. Yet characteristically, even here Tennyson, a child of his time, is unwilling to give way to absolute nihilism, and the poem snatches a kind of victory from the jaws of defeat:

> Peace, let it be! for I loved him, and love him for ever: the
> dead are not dead but alive.

Whilst this downward movement towards death and oblivion is a genuine and potent strand in the poetry, overall it is equally valid to see Tennyson as a pre-Darwinian evolutionist who expresses a positive response to contemporary science, and who reads evolution as teleological in direction. The poet is sceptical about the atheistic tendencies in geological writers like Lyell and Mantell; in other theorists like Paley and Whewell, Tennyson discerned an autonomous universe which aligned itself with a beneficent deity. *In Memoriam*, in its scope and reach, nicely expounds the poet's deep commitment to gradualism and change as the key to life. The speaker's feelings change over a period of time from grief to reconciliation, just as his feelings about the geological record change from fear and doubt towards an acceptance of the order opened up by the new investigations. Towards the beginning of the poem, in one of the early lyrics, the text longs for fixity:

> I held it truth, with him who sings
>   To one clear harp in divers tones,
>   That men may rise on stepping-stones
> Of their dead selves to higher things.

(1)

But as yet there is little faith in gradualism and progress, and the poet is far from reconciled to loss; on the contrary, the poem insists, time will simply obliterate his love and faith. When looked at from this perspective, the universe becomes like a dead machine:

> O Sorrow, cruel fellowship,
>   O Priestess in the vaults of Death,
>   O sweet and bitter in a breath,
> What whispers from thy lying lip?

'The stars,' she whispers, 'blindly run;
    A web is wov'n across the sky;
    From out waste places comes a cry,
And murmurs from the dying sun:

                                                      (3)

Although this message emanates, we are told, from 'lying lips', the sense of panic and emptiness brought on by the new science reaches its climax later, in sections 55 and 56. Man, it seems here, is not part of a universal harmony; he is a discord, and the fossil record shows predictively how types and species will disappear in the long evolutionary perspectives:

    Are God and Nature then at strife,
        That Nature lends such evil dreams?
        So careful of the type she seems,
    So careless of the single life;

The poet staggers under the weight of his speculations (55), faltering 'where I firmly trod'. In a natural world 'red in tooth and claw' (56), it becomes appallingly evident that man may disappear just as did the dinosaur; the person who, like Hallam, 'battled for the True, the Just' will 'Be blown about the desert dust/ Or seal'd within the iron hills' (*ibid.*). This is the nadir of the poem's evolutionary meditations. Gradually, the reader senses that love of Hallam, and through him of God, gains independence from this bleak scientism. A more stable and positive sense of order prevails through acceptance of the permanence of change. At the level of natural phenomena, the poet reflects, all is change: 'The hills are shadows, and they flow/ From form to form'. The sense of process is central to this concept: Lyell's thesis had supposed a law or end towards which all causation pointed, and it is within this theology that Hallam is finally placed:

    Who throve and branch'd from clime to clime,
        The herald of a higher race,
        And of himself in higher place,
    If so he type this work of time.

                                     (118)

Whilst Tennyson's scientific speculations are often thought to be proof of his modernity, his desire to keep abreast of the advanced thinking of his age, they may also be part and parcel of his political caution and conservatism. His vision of evolution is providential and gradualist, and smoothly blind to the shocks and dislocations of contemporary history. A seamless view of past and present protects the poet from a full facing up to the issues of an industrial society in turmoil, or a rendering of the sharp breaks in the 'text' of history which the rebellions throughout Europe signalled within the period. Such turning away is probably psychological in origin: there is in Tennyson a dread and fascination about the unplumbed depths of the psyche. For the modern reader, this is perhaps one of the most interesting aspects of the poet's work. Inward communing leads to a sense of impotent incapacity for action, that very incapacity which motivates some of his most successful poems, and which seems to derive from the Larkinesque 'desire for oblivion'. Tennyson will beautifully objectify this mood in landscape, as he does, for instance, in 'The Last Tournament':

> ... as the crest of some slow-arching wave,
> Heard in dead night along that table-shore,
> Drops flat, and after the great waters break
> Whitening for half a league, and thin themselves,
> Far over sands marbled with moon and cloud,
> From less and less to nothing;

This sense of the dwindling away of the perceived world, and of the self, is archetypal: this is the poetry of a man who remains radically uncertain that his poetry is an accurate mirror of his experience. The knowledge of the chaos, energy and confusion of the Victorian world exemplified in Dickens's novels, for instance, is inimical to Tennyson's cultivation of the long perspective. The poetry is produced out of his desire for a certainty which he acknowledged as impossible of attainment, and in that sense Tennyson was indeed a true Victorian.

# 3. The Tennysonian Poetic

In a letter to his friend A. W. M. Baillie, written in September 1864 when the Poet Laureate was at the height of his fame, the Catholic poet Gerard Manley Hopkins announced that he had 'begun to *doubt* Tennyson'.[1] This doubt was set off, he revealed, by his reading the recently published *Enoch Arden and Other Poems*, a reading which led Hopkins to postulate a thesis about the nature of poetic language which is of peculiar relevance to the reader of Tennyson. According to this critical argument, the language of verse may be divided into differing kinds. First, Hopkins argues, comes the highest style, 'the language of inspiration', which is generated by 'a mood of great, abnormal . . . mental acuteness'. The second level Hopkins designates 'Parnassian', a type of verse issuing '*on and from the level* of a poet's mind, not, as in the other case, when the inspiration, which is the gift of genius, raises him above himself'. Parnassian language, we gather, 'does not sing . . . in its flights'. 'In a poet's particular kind of Parnassian lies most of his style, of his manner, of his mannerism.' Hopkins cites as an instance of Parnassian verse the description of Enoch Arden's tropical island:

> The lightning flash of insect and of bird,
> The lustre of the long convolvuluses
> That coil'd around the stately stems,

This is Parnassian, Hopkins would urge, because it fails to take the reader by surprise; on the contrary, the reader feels that if she were to write, then this is the kind of verse she herself would compose. When a poet 'palls' on the reader, Hopkins believes, it is because of this Parnassian strain which runs 'in an intelligibly laid down path'. Shakespeare, he argues, exemplifies a poet virtually free from this strain, whilst Wordsworth is an example of someone writing, in Hopkins's phrase, 'such an intolerable deal of Parnassian'. Tennyson is 'Tennysonian' when he lapses into this almost somnambulistic utterance; but Hopkins allows that he achieves elsewhere effects which are 'divine, terribly beautiful'.

Hopkins's categories are worth pondering by the reader of Tennyson, since they offer a way of distinguishing those poems or parts of poems which are characteristic of the first order, and those passages which are distinctly 'Tennysonian', written as if for easy readerly consumption.

A valuable starting point for the discussion of Tennyson's style is still

Arthur Hallam's review of the *Poems, Chiefly Lyrical* (1830) which
appeared in the *Englishman's Magazine* in August 1831. During his time
as an Apostle at Cambridge, and up to his death in 1833, Hallam was
preoccupied with moral and aesthetic questions, and his position was
certainly that adopted by his friend in his writing up to the middle of his
career, when overtly philosophical questions begin to be more fully can-
vassed. The chief end of poetry, Hallam argues, is aesthetic: wherever
anything other than the 'desire for beauty' predominates in the creative
mind, 'the result is false in art'.[2] Hallam argues that the reasoning
faculty is, if not anathema to poetic creation, at least to be held in
abeyance if the result is to 'enrapture' its audience. Hallam writes that
after the impact of Romanticism:

Those different powers of poetic disposition, the energies of Sensitive, of Reflective,
of Passionate Emotion, which in former times were intermingled, and derived from
mutual support an extensive empire over the feelings of men, were now restrained
within separate spheres of agency. The whole system no longer worked har-
moniously, and by intrinsic harmony acquired external freedom; but there arose a
violent and unusual action in the several component functions, each for itself, all
striving to reproduce the regular power which the whole had once enjoyed.

T. S. Eliot's thesis of a dissociation of sensibility dating from the early
seventeenth century led towards the creation of a symbolist poetic in
which discursive content is minimal, and Arthur Hallam seems to be
pointing the way here towards that central aesthetic project of modern-
ism. Ideas, that is to say, have a place in poetry only as sensations, and it
is the priority given to image and sensation which leads Hallam to value
the second generation of Romantics, Keats, Byron and Shelley, over the
first generation, dominated by Wordsworth. Both Keats and Shelley, it
is claimed, are 'poets of sensation rather than reflection'. Such poets live
'in a world of images', hence inevitably they are not 'descriptive' but
'picturesque'. Hallam describes the characteristic poetic sensibility of
Keats and Shelley thus:

Susceptible of the slightest impulse from external nature, their fine organs
trembled into emotion at colours, and sounds, and movements, unperceived or
unregarded by duller temperaments. Rich and clear were their perceptions of
visible forms; full and deep their feelings of music. So vivid was the delight
attending the simple exertions of eye and ear, that it became mingled more and
more with their trains of active thought, and tended to absorb their whole being
into the energy of sense. Other poets *seek* for images to illustrate their conceptions;
these men had no need to seek; they lived in a world of images; for the most
important and extensive portion of their life consisted in those emotions, which
are immediately consonant with sensation.

The poet, in this account, is moving towards the kind of synaesthesia which was to be adumbrated in Baudelaire's theory of correspondence, and many of Tennyson's earliest poems do exhibit synaesthetic properties. The eighteenth-century cult of the picturesque in landscape, and later in landscape painting, is adduced as a vital part of the poet's sensibility. The aim is therefore, through sense impressions, to attain moments of heightened and intense perception and awareness, moments gained by those 'whose poetry is a sort of magic'. Working against such magic, Hallam perceives, is the 'diffusion of machinery' in the early Victorian period. As a result, there will be a necessary 'decrease of *subjective* power, arising from a prevalence of social activity, and a continual absorption of the higher feelings into the palpable interests of ordinary life'. Hallam insists upon a poetry of suggestiveness and symbol, rather than what he regards as the characteristically Wordsworthian poetry of statement. He proceeds, in the course of the review, to insert his friend into his definition of the poetic with persuasive ease. According to the categories expounded by Hallam, Tennyson possesses the five primary qualities of the great poet. First, a luxuriance of imagination combined with 'control'; secondly, a power of embodying his feelings in 'moods of character'; thirdly, a 'picturesque delineation of objects'; fourthly, rhythmic and stanzaic variety; and fifthly, 'elevated habits of thought'. Thus the work of Tennyson is to be valued for its sensitivity to landscape and feeling, and these are hailed as the hallmarks of modern literature. As Hallam wrote to Tennyson: 'You and I are conversant about the same subjects, you as poet, I in the humbler station as critic; to converse together upon them will be all the better for my criticism and perhaps for your poetry.'

Hallam's essay reveals a profound grasp of the potency which landscape description could have in creating an interior landscape of the mind, and of the way Victorian poetry worked to create its objective correlatives. The Victorians slowly lost the Romantic intuition of a perfect 'fit' between mind and nature, and this loss is recorded in the habit, notable in the Pre-Raphaelites, of conveying states of mind through imaginary landscapes. There is thus a curious conjunction in such art of precisely observed minutiae and imaginary setting, and it was this conjunction which would lead, at the turn of the century, into symbolism and imagism. In 'Mariana', for instance, Tennyson gives the reader a scene endowed with almost photographic immediacy:

> All day within the dreamy house,
> The doors upon their hinges creak'd;

> The blue fly sung in the pane; the mouse
> > Behind the mouldering wainscot shriek'd,
> Or from the crevice peer'd about.

The catalogue of precisely rendered detail is specifically mobilized to convey to the reader a sense of desolation and ennui: this is essentially a landscape perceived by the silent heroine. John Stuart Mill, in another review of the early poetry, remarked upon Tennyson's power of creating scenery in keeping with a certain state of human feeling, 'so fitted to it as to be the embodied symbol of it, and to summon up the state of feeling itself, with a force not to be surpassed by anything but reality'.

The poetic mind as it were creates what it perceives, and yet the poetry is anchored in a naturalistically accurate mode of sights and sounds. Sound effect and repetition, indeed, play a vital part in such poetry, as Hallam noted when he argued that the 'tone becomes the sign of the feeling; and they reciprocally suggest each other'. Language thus becomes a sign or a sound which evokes an emotional complex not expressible otherwise than through onomatopoeic suggestion. 'Sound conveys meaning where words do not,' Hallam suggested, and this touches upon an acute problem for the reader of Tennyson. The poetry, especially the early work, seems to embody two contradictory views of language: the first, that words are mere counters, almost incapable of reproducing sense experience; the second, that language operates in a magical way as a kind of incantation. The deconstructive dangers of an extreme aestheticism, which were not avoided by many of Tennyson's disciples, were perhaps what led the poet outwards in his middle period towards the form of the dramatic monologue, where extremes of subjectivity could be given an objective frame.

Fidelity and accuracy in the poetry work, in Hallam's view, to produce a satisfying intensity of response in the reading mind. It is this intensity which Tennyson often seeks in an artistic project which unsettles the Wordsworthian commitment to a preordained fitting together of mind and external world in educative harmony. The most potent of Tennyson's texts express the plight of individual consciousness bereft of that seminal Romantic sense of harmony, a plight which is traceable both in Tennyson's generalized optimism and in his more personal pessimism, a melancholy fixation with a prolonging of the aesthetic moment into poetic ecstasy. The most successful poems, it might be urged, are those which capture such moments – 'Mariana', 'The Lady of Shalott', and so on; less successful generally are the attempts at a framing narrative, such as 'Oenone' or 'Locksley Hall'. The sensibility revealed in the poems is a

delicate one, prone to insecurity, fear and doubt. The 'black blood' of
the Tennysons expressed itself, not in the breakdown which afflicted so
many of his brothers, but in a poetry in which the individual's sense of
identity is precariously held.

The isolation of Somersby in the poet's formative years was com-
pounded by his extreme short-sightedness. A friend recalled of Tennyson,
'The shortness of his sight, which was extreme, tormented him always.
When he was looking at any object he seemed to be smelling it.' Such a
degree of myopia had its compensations: it pays dividends in many
poems in the attention to detail, light, shape and colour:

> About a stone-cast from the wall
>     A sluice with blacken'd waters slept,
> And o'er it many, round and small,
>     The cluster'd marish-mosses crept.

('Mariana')

That which is close at hand is very intimately felt in such lines, whilst
that which is distant is lost in vague immensity, stretching away like the
Lincolnshire marsh below the Wolds:

> Hard by a poplar shook alway,
>     All silver-green with gnarlèd bark:
>     For leagues no other tree did mark
> The level waste, the rounding gray.

(*ibid.*)

In many poems we may detect a strangely dialectical movement between vivid immediacy and a sense of the vast. In an early poem, 'Ar-
mageddon', the poet reflects on how 'Each failing sense,/ As with a
momentary flash of light,/ Grew thrillingly distinct and keen'. In such a
state he 'saw/ The smallest grain that dappled the dark Earth,/ The
indistinctest atom in deep air'. But this distinctiveness will always allow
the poet to lose himself in the indistinct:

> All sense of Time
> And Being and Place was swallowed up and lost
> Within a victory of boundless thought.
> I was a part of the Unchangeable
> A scintillation of Eternal Mind,
> Remix'd and burning with its parent fire.

The reciprocity between the poet and a vivid and somewhat unstably
conceived nature led towards what W. H. Auden designated a 'vertigo of

anxiety', trance-like states which were essential to the Tennysonian poetic process. Nature attracts Tennyson in its minutiae, but also in its flowing changeability. Water, rivers and the sea are significant emblems in such poetry, as is the shifting play of light upon landscape which is so characteristic of the sky-dominated landscapes of his native county. The poetry often exerts its power to transmute the seemingly ordinary manifestations of English scenery into something strange and exotic: the land of the Lotos-Eaters, for instance, owed much to a visit to Torquay, and the haunting Arthurian 'last great battle in the west' drew its resonance from childhood memories of the Lincolnshire coast. There is frequently a pattern in the poems which moves from the familiar, through an almost hypnotic vividness of perception, towards something richly unsettling. In the early 'Song', for example, the iterative rhythmic and rhyming effects allow the autumnal garden to take on a peculiar life of its own, which disturbs the elegiac note:

> Heavily hangs the broad sunflower
> Over its grave i' the earth so chilly;
> Heavily hangs the hollyhock,
> Heavily hangs the tiger-lily.

A poem like 'A Dream of Fair Women' takes this process further. Here the speaker enters a world of dreams which relieves him of his personal anxieties: the 'smell of violets, hidden in the green' flows into his 'empty soul' in blissful innocence. There is an underlying desire here for what Freud would designate the 'oceanic feeling' of a kind of return to the womb, a return which is also imagined in a group of revealing sea-poems, 'The Sea Fairies', 'The Mermaid', and 'The Merman', whose song seems to have been overheard by Eliot's Prufrock:

> . . . at night I would roam abroad and play
> With the mermaids in and out of the rocks,
> Dressing their hair with the white sea-flower;
> And holding them back by their flowing locks
> I would kiss them often under the sea,
> And kiss them again till they kiss'd me
> Laughingly, laughingly;

If such poems articulate something of the libidinous free flow of desire so markedly censored in Victorian literature, they also offer a tempting fantasy of escape for the self. The desire to escape this self, and the equally strong desire to hold on to it, simultaneously energize the contradictions which are at the centre of Tennyson's poetic power.

The specifically Tennysonian style issues, then, from a divided sensibility.

Many of the poems, indeed, are characterized by duality. The contrast in some of the nature poetry between microcosm and macrocosm, for instance, may well reflect a division between a 'public' and a 'private' self. Even work in the early *Poems by Two Brothers* expresses and explores this dualism:

> Why should we weep for those who die?
> They fall – their dust returns to dust;
> Their souls shall live eternally
> Within the mansions of the just.
> They die to live, they sink to rise.
>
> ('Why should we weep?')

The Cambridge prize-poem 'Timbuctoo' offers many examples of this mode of utterance. The ostensible subject of the exercise is clearly a vehicle which the poet uses to meditate upon the differing claims of fact and imagination. A spirit shows the poet a vision of the fabled city, 'A wilderness of spires, and chrystal pile/ Of rampart upon rampart, dome on dome', but goes on to warn: 'the time is well-nigh come/ When I must render up this glorious home'. In a moment the 'brilliant towers . . . darken', 'shrink and shiver into huts,/ Black specks amid a waste of dreary sand'. Yet the spirit remains the tutelary angel of 'the great vine of Fable'. The poet and the positivist seeker after factual information discover both in interaction, in a Keatsian sense of the dialectic between fact and imagination. Another early poem, 'The Mystic', delineates a sage who lives in the constant realm of 'serene abstraction', and Οἱ ῥέοντες affirms that 'All thoughts, all creeds, all dreams are true'.

In 'Dualisms' the children singing in the meadow, 'Like, unlike, they sing together/ Side by side' – neatly express the merging of contraries. These contrasts meet most potently, perhaps, in a late poem, 'Lucretius', where the philosopher feels tragically unable to cope with the contrariety of life. In his monologue Lucretius expounds a set of apparent antitheses, but constantly searches for a way to reduce multiplicity to a single determinative principle. Paradoxically, this demand for a logical pattern for existence produces chaos. Lucretius sees that nature emerges 'balmier and nobler from her bath of storm', but fails to apply this to himself since he has already ascribed a negative value to the passions. The result is that in the conclusion the philosopher is drawn inexorably towards suicide as the solution to his sense of confusion. The poem begins with a prologue, in which Lucretius turns from the embrace of his wife Lucilia to 'those three hundred scrolls/ Left by the Teacher, whom he held divine'. His wife administers an aphrodisiac in an effort to release her husband's repressed passions, but this leads to the philosopher recounting several disturbing dream sequences. In one, nature is revealed as a nightmare of chaos, in which 'flaring atom-streams' and 'torrents of her myriad universe' fly on 'to clash together again'.

Another vision is suggestively Freudian:

> Then, then, from utter gloom stood out the breasts,
> The breasts of Helen, and hoveringly a sword
> Now over and now under, now direct,
> Pointed itself to pierce, but sank down shamed
> At all that beauty;

This terrible beauty renders impotent the force which opposes it, and thus calms the philosopher so that he is more attuned to seeking understanding on an abstract plane. Yet this recourse to rationality is constantly undermined by memories of recent temptation, a dislocation of the claims of science which leads inexorably towards dissolution: 'I often grew/ Tired of so much within our little life,/ Or of so little in our little life'. Lucretius finally plunges the dagger into his side: his answer to the contrarieties which have so deceived and plagued him is to seek the unanimity of death. Whilst 'Lucretius' is not one of Tennyson's finest poems, it is highly symptomatic of a divided consciousness in its creator, and its movement of falling away from the perplexities of life is enacted again and again in his texts, and nowhere more productively than in the dramatic monologues.

The American critic Robert Langbaum has argued [3] that the dramatic monologue originated as a poetic form when the Victorian poet invented a lyric based upon experiences which are not his or her own, and that this produced a disequilibrium between concept and experience. The dramatic monologue in which the poet inhabits the persona, or adopts the mask, of an alien being, forces upon the reader, Langbaum suggests, a conflict between sympathy and dispassionate judgement. This conflict may flow from the Romantic conviction that imaginative and sense experience is primary and direct whilst analytic reflection is secondary and problematical. There are, nevertheless, significant differences between the strategies of the Romantic lyricist and the Victorian monologuist: the poet who creates the monologue withdraws from the utterance, thereby evading his or her own experiences in any direct form. The reader of the great monologues of Browning or Tennyson, or of their modernist inheritors such as Eliot or Pound, is conscious of the craftsman's skill. The poem is in a very real sense a brilliant *performance*, and one which depends greatly upon conjuring a specifically heard voice. The kind of status to which such poetry aspires is ambivalent: the monologue form suggests that all experience is personal and relative, based on individual mood and perception, but also implies that its content does not rely upon the nature of its creator. The monologue emphasizes the personal nature of 'truth' and 'reality', whilst striving to transcend that relativity by separating the utterance from the poet's own experience. A tension is thereby set up between the poem as personal creation and the text as object.

Tennyson derives strength and variety from this tension, and utilizes the form in a manner markedly different from his great rival, Robert Browning. From the time of his earliest effusions, such as 'Memory' and 'Antony to Cleopatra', Tennyson enjoyed the donning of a mask. He delighted in the type of classical rhetoric whereby the writer imagined what a particular character might have said or thought upon a specific occasion, and united this ploy with the Victorian notion of the 'mono-drama', in which a range of feelings is created through linguistic invention. Tennyson tends to explore, not the great individuals of the Browning monologues, but certain states of mind and feeling. His characters frequently emanate from myth rather than history, as is the case with Browning. Extreme states, in St Simeon or the speaker of *Maud*, lead to a kind of dissociation effect which achieves a different kind of irony from Browning's personae. Each of his most powerful monologuists – Ulysses, Tithonus, the Lotos-Eaters, St Simeon, the hero of *Maud* – are cut off in some way from their fellows by the intensity or peculiarity of their feelings. The Tennysonian monologue, therefore, expresses and enacts a kind of pessimism about the prospects of useful intercourse between the speaker and the rest of humanity. Tithonus is anguished at being cut off, like Yeats in 'Sailing to Byzantium', from the world of the young; the Lotos-Eaters fear that 'our household hearths are cold'; Ulysses ends the first part of his monologue with the thought that his people 'know not me'; and the speaker in *Maud* despairs at his alienation from 'a world in which I have hardly mixed'. Such figures – and they are some of Tennyson's most characteristic – are subtly poised between life and an extinction which is felt as both threat and attraction. In the imagining and framing of extreme utterance, Tennyson achieves in these poems a rare universality of statement.

Although the young Tennyson worshipped Lord Byron, the true begetters of the early *Poems by Two Brothers* are the mid-Augustan nature poets such as Gray and Thomson. The rhetoric of the early political poems finds its source in the eighteenth-century habit of addressing

abstract questions, and this rhetoric sits uneasily with the more characteristically Tennysonian obsession with detail and sound effect:

> Her song the lintwhite swelleth,
> The clear-voiced mavis dwelleth,
>   The callow throstle lispeth,
> The slumbrous wave outwelleth,
>   The babbling runnel crispeth,
> The hollow grot replieth
>   Where Claribel low-lieth.

('Claribel')

There is a potent dropping away here in the sound and rhythm, and a
kind of somnambulistic lapsing out into a state of near insensibility. The
verse moves beyond pure descriptiveness towards the kind of 'pathetic
fallacy' later defined by Ruskin, in which landscape both communicates,
and is drenched in, an emotional charge. Some of the consonantal repetition of 'm' and 's' sounds works to produce a feeling of sensuous
relaxation. In such a work Tennyson already begins to experiment with
making the natural world act symbolically within the text. Images begin
to resonate with carefully calculated and yet indefinable meanings and
associations. Such sophisticated symbolization would serve the poet well
in the major poems composed in the later 1830s, such as 'Morte
d'Arthur', and many of the landscape passages of *In Memoriam*. The
technique may be exposed in a less well-known poem, 'Isabel'. The poet
somewhat smugly describes Isabel as a paragon of wifely virtue, but in
the final stanza suggestion replaces statement to create a deeper complexity of utterance:

> The mellow'd reflex of a winter moon;
> A clear stream flowing with a muddy one,
>   Till in its onward current it absorbs
>   With swifter movement and in purer light
>   The vexèd eddies of its wayward brother:

The image of the winter moon serves to suggest a cool chastity, but
that coolness is nicely tempered by the adjective 'mellow'd'; the following
lines place this image against that of the clinging vine as an emblem of
fidelity. The probability that this is a portrait of the poet's mother,
whose 'clear stream' was compelled to mingle with the 'muddy one' of
Dr Tennyson, may not wholly exonerate the poem from a feminist
interrogation of its dominatingly patriarchal ideology. Nevertheless, it is
a characteristic transposition of human relations into the realm of nature,

and it sets up a pattern which was to recur with Tennyson in more ambitious works.

To revert for a moment to Hopkins's distinction between kinds of poetic image, it is evident that Tennyson is, at his best, a poet whose gifts are often onomatopoeically preconscious and 'inspirational', and at his second-best distinctly 'Parnassian'. There is a good deal of evidence that Tennyson's mind was often possessed by sounds in themselves. 'When I was eight,' he recalled, 'I remember making a line I thought grander than Campbell, or Byron, or Scott. I rolled it out, it was this: "With slaughterous sons of thunder rolled the flood" – a great nonsense, of course, but I thought it fine.' This emphasis upon musicality of effect is behind the Laureate's famous stricture upon his rival, Robert Browning, who 'has plenty of music in him, but . . . cannot get it out'. Tennyson's creative process seems to have centred around a struggle to produce a verbal sequence which sounds beautiful and to arrange it rhythmically. This notably unmusical man paradoxically contrived to evolve a highly musical verse. Because of his unhappy childhood Tennyson seems to have turned away from persons and relationships towards the landscape, and to have utilized nature both as a substitute for relationships and as a source of symbolism. He once characterized his beloved Virgil as 'land-scape-lover, lord of language', and it may be that his own style has its roots in such a classical model.

In the process of composition Tennyson often relied upon a seminal phrase which would then trigger the creative act. Hallam Tennyson commented, 'My father's poems were generally based upon some single phrase like "Someone had blundered": and were rolled about, so to speak, in his head, before he wrote them down.' F.T. Palgrave, a close confidant of the poet and editor of the popular *Golden Treasury of Verse*, wrote at greater length on this process:

more than once he said that his poems sprang often from a 'nucleus'; some one word, may be, or brief melodious phrase which had floated through the brain, as it were unbidden. And perhaps at once whilst walking they were presently wrought into a little song. But if he did not write it down on the spot, the lyric fled from him irrecoverably.

The profitable creative expansion of such a nucleus often depends, in Tennyson as in other poets, upon an element of 'intertextuality' – a conscious or, more frequently unconscious, recall of earlier texts which now, subtly transmuted, inhabit the Tennysonian text. His poems resonate with memories of Virgil and Homer, Shakespeare, Keats and Shelley. The weight and richness of this residue is so great that Tennyson was often charged with plagiarism. The Laureate was, for instance, deeply stung when Churton Collins described his work as 'of an essentially reflective character' and ambiguously praised his 'assimilative skill'. As Christopher Ricks has shown, some of Tennyson's finest effects were produced through self-plagiarism. The lines 'To follow knowledge like a sinking star/ Beyond the utmost bound of human thought', which now appear in 'Ulysses', originally came from a poem called 'Tiresias'. Ricks argues that such self-borrowings relate to the obsessive concern of the poet with the passage of time, and acutely suggests that in a world of flux Tennyson found a 'rallying-point' in the continuity of his own creativity.[4] Indeed, such self-borrowing may point to a desire to find a wholeness and continuum which is safe from the depredations of time.

One aspect of Tennyson's creative imagination which remains mysterious is his possibly epileptic susceptibility to states of trance. He could, a friend recalled, fall into such a trance 'by thinking intently of his own name'; the poet described this power, which he had possessed since early childhood, in 'The Ancient Sage' of 1885:

> 'for more than once when I
> Sat all alone, revolving in myself
> The word that is the symbol of myself,
> The mortal limit of the Self was loosed,
> And past into the Nameless, as a cloud
> Melts into Heaven.'

In a poem from the other end of his career Tennyson noted how a sense of the intimate detail of nature could serve as a prelude to a sense of access into infinity, a state when, as the poet declares, 'I wondered with deep wonder'. The ability to go out of the body creates, in the verse, both anxiety and rapture, as in the famous vision of Arthur Hallam in *In Memoriam*, section 95. The feeling in such passages of a realm beneath and beyond the phenomenal world is crucial in the Tennysonian poetic. But such an experience also presents dangers, as in the Prince's trances in *The Princess*. The fear attendant upon the loss of self, and the uncertainties attendant upon creativity, are undercurrents in Tennyson's oeuvre as a whole. Tennyson is crucially a poet, not of Victorian certitude, but of a precariously held selfhood created in defiance of his age.

The dialectically held and opposing tendencies in Tennyson's poetry are already self-evident in 'The Two Voices', with its dramatic exploration of the effects of a divided will. Although the voice of positive faith finally carries the day, it is the nagging voice of doubt which has the best tunes. Having lost his religious faith the poet no longer sees the value in devoting his life to the service of mankind, and in the first voice he imagines a mockery of all those spiritual values which were to feed the Victorian age:

> 'Much less this dreamer, deaf and blind,
> Named man, may hope some truth to find,
> That bears relation to the mind.
>
> 'For every worm beneath the moon
> Draws different threads, and late and soon
> Spins, toiling out his own cocoon.'

Suicidal despair leads the poet to seek to oppose this tempter by appealing to the imagination's 'mystic gleams', but a safe haven is only reached through the observation of the pious church-going family:

> These three made unity so sweet,
> My frozen heart began to beat,
> Remembering its ancient heat.
>
> I blest them, and they wander'd on:
> I spoke, but answer came there none:
> The dull and bitter voice was gone.
>
> A second voice was at mine ear,
> A little whisper silver-clear,
> A murmur, 'Be of better cheer.'

But such social engagement is often more ambivalently imagined, in 'The Lady of Shalott', 'The Lotos-Eaters', and elsewhere, and Pallas Athene's instructions in 'Oenone' lay bare the dangerous temptations of a collapse of the will: the goddess there claims that 'Self-reverence, self-knowledge, self-control' alone 'lead life to sovereign power'.

A similar note resounds through 'The Palace of Art', which seeks to refute the hypnotically egocentric delights of art for art's sake. The soul's idea in alienating itself from the world is one of disdain for humanity:

> 'O God-like isolation which art mine,
>   I can but count thee perfect gain,
> What time I watch the darkening droves of swine
>   That range on yonder plain.'

From the 1842 volumes onwards Tennyson began uneasily to assume his more overtly Victorian guise. The note of self-division persists, but is subsumed, as in 'Locksley Hall', within a larger sense of social implication expressed through a melodramatic plot involving lovers of differing class positions. After rejecting the temptation to sensual forgetfulness on an island, the hero characteristically embraces a future dominated by change, celebrating the superiority of European progress to a 'cycle of Cathay'.

There are clearly far more 'consumable' poems in the 1842 collection, which includes such narrative efforts as 'The Gardener's Daughter', 'Audley Court', 'Walking to the Mail' and 'Edward Gray'. Tennyson has moved from the private communings of some of the most potent of the poems of the 1830s to the vision of social progress outlined in 'Morte d'Arthur', 'Locksley Hall' and elsewhere, and to a Ruskinian perspective on the communal uses of the aesthetic. Princess Ida, for instance, has certainly been reading her Ruskin attentively. Yet as Tennyson grew closer to the establishment of his day, his doubts lingered. 'Will Waterproof's Lyrical Monologue' gives voice to some of those doubts; the speaker talks feelingly of:

> Hours, when the Poet's words and looks
>   Had yet their native glow:
> Nor yet the fear of little books
>   Had made him talk for show;

With 'Enoch Arden' and the *Idylls*, the 'public' Tennyson reaches his peak, or his nadir, according to the reader's view. The *Idylls* notoriously display many of those qualities felt to be characteristically 'Victorian': a morally earnest hero, whose ideal society is undermined by illicit passion. Although the poems purport to delineate an ideal past, there is a somewhat doom-laden atmosphere throughout, coupled with an unsettling sense of moral ambiguity which undercuts the proclaimed certainties. Indeed, the very legitimacy of Arthur's claim to the throne is dubious, and this equivocation ramifies into the moral structure of the series. In the picture of the last great battle in the west, the misty and shadowy landscape comes to symbolize the misgivings within the Round Table itself and epitomizes those questions of appearance and reality which have dogged Tennyson's career. In the late work the tone of pessimism increases. The challenging tone of 'Locksley Hall' gives way to the petulant questioning of 'Locksley Hall Sixty Years After', where belief and faith in progress are angrily dismantled. This belief and faith are transmuted now into a search for a spiritual realm outside time, in such poems as 'The Ancient Sage' and 'Vastness', where a quest for transcendence is fuelled alike by the poet's age, and by his deepening despair about his own society. The stark disparity is acutely revealed in one of the most seminal of these late poems, 'Merlin and the Gleam', where actual and ideal collide with a painful and memorable intensity. Here the faith in progress, the upward momentum of the Victorian age, finally collapses in wintry discontent: and that momentum is mysteriously and ruinously implicated in the poet's loss of inspiration:

> Clouds and darkness
> Closed upon Camelot;
> Arthur had vanish'd
> I knew not whither,
> The king who loved me,
> And cannot die;

The reader who seeks the roots of the Tennysonian poetic, however, may fruitfully turn to the early work. In 1835 his friend James Spedding remarked that Tennyson was 'a man always discontented with the Present till it has become the Past, and then he yearns towards it and worships it, and not only worships it, but is discontented because it is past'. This motiveless melancholia certainly generates some of the finest poems, as T. S. Eliot noticed when he observed in Tennyson 'emotion so deeply suppressed, even from himself, as to tend rather towards the blackest melancholia than towards dramatic action'. There is a potent mixture of dream, memory and desire which is in conflict with fear and conscience, for example in the very early 'In Deep and Solemn Dreams'. The Dreamer meets 'sunny faces of lost days . . . Forms which live but in the mind':

> And we speak as we have spoken
> Ere our love by death was broken.

But at dawn a breeze breaks the spell of 'tearless sleep':

> Dear lips, loved eyes, ye fade, ye fly,
> Even in my fear ye die,
> And the hollow dark I dread
> Closes round my friendless head.

In another unpublished early poem, 'Sense and Conscience', Tennyson deals directly with this theme. Conscience is quieted by the powers of 'sense' (sensuality) in a bower of 'pleasurable flowers'. The poet is prey to some 'delicious dreams' and 'witching fantasies', until memory awakes him:

> ... Rage seized upon him then
> And grasping with both palms his wondrous blade,
> Sheer through the summit of the tallest flowers
> He drave it ...

As a result of this violent, and curiously erotic, action:

> ... The ivy from the stem
> Was torn, the vine made desolate; his feet
> Were crimson'd with its blood, from which flows joy
> And bitterness, first joy from bitterness,
> And then again great bitterness from joy.

Thus to deny the senses leads towards repression and suffering. Tennyson, even as a young man, frequently calls up what has been termed the 'mask of age', in order to transmute desire and anxiety into loss and memory. This allows him a gain in objectivity and unity within the poem, where inner and outer worlds unite in an aesthetic whole. Both *Poems, Chiefly Lyrical* (1830) and *Poems* (1833) display this pattern of creation. In 'Recollections of the Arabian Nights' the poet voyages through a sub-tropical paradise and dreams that he hears a nightingale:

> Not he: but something which possess'd
> The darkness of the world, delight,
> Life, anguish, death, immortal love,
> Ceasing not, mingled, unrepress'd,
>   Apart from place, withholding time,
>   But flattering the golden prime
>   Of good Haroun Alraschid.

An entranced vision of an 'amorous' Persian girl follows, and the poem closes with sleep. 'A Dream of Fair Women' is rather more ambitious than this sub-Keatsian exercise. In this text, images of war and action are the prelude to a forest scene of sleep and dreaming:

> The smell of violets, hidden in the green,
>   Pour'd back into my empty soul and frame
> The times when I remember to have been
>   Joyful and free from blame.

The poet perceives a sequence of famous women of the past, and the poem again concludes in a dawn scene.

That note of regressive withdrawal from the world will resound throughout the later work. In *The Princess*, for instance, the 'amorous'

Prince disguises himself as a woman in order to gain entry to the cloistered college presided over by Princess Ida. When he fights to gain Ida's favour he is wounded, and characteristically falls 'silent in the muffled cage of life', only to be nursed back to life by Ida herself.

All these fantasies of withdrawal and loss came starkly to life with the death of Hallam, and it is a pattern of behaviour which *In Memoriam* minutely records with great fidelity. The poem releases many of the themes of deepest concern to the poet: longing and frustration; the mask of age; sceptical doubt; the role of the artist in society; the evolutionary principle; the clash between social order and inner disorder. This poem, and much that is central in the Tennysonian canon, mirrors Freud's notion that melancholia is related to an unconscious loss of love-object. In this respect, as in many others, 'The Ancient Sage' epitomizes and sums up a lifetime's poetic obsessions:

> Today? but what of yesterday? for oft
> On me, when boy, there came what then I call'd,
> Who knew no books and no philosophies,
> In my boy-phrase 'The Passion of the Past',
> The first gray streak of earliest summer-dawn,
> The last long stripe of waning crimson gloom,
> As if the late and early were but one –
> A height, a broken grange, a grove, a flower
> Had murmurs 'Lost and gone and lost and gone!'

# 4. Early Poems (1830, 1832)

## 'Mariana' (1830)

Tennyson disclosed that the location of this poem was 'no particular grange, but one which rose to the music of Shakespeare's words'. He prefixed at the head of the poem the suggestive epigraph 'Mariana in the moated grange', which is a slight misquotation of a line from Shakespeare's *Measure for Measure*: 'There, at the moated grange, resides this dejected Mariana' (III.i). The grange, with its 'rusted nails', surrounded by the 'glooming flats' of the Lincolnshire landscape, appears as almost a manifestation of the consciousness of the heroine. Indeed, it was Tennyson's achievement to have created this powerfully passive image of the 'feminine' for Victorian poetry and art. There is a highly wrought interplay between the narrative voice and the voice of Mariana herself, caught only in the refrain, the effect being to bring the reader close to, yet not identical with, the girl's experience (or its absence). The images of physical brokenness and decay become emblems of the mind here, and there is a strong evocation of the painfully slow passage of time. The poem is a statement of immobility and frustration, themes which were to become hallmarks of Tennyson's art, and the desperation felt in the persona is registered in the atomistic sense of detail – here is a world which is no longer held together by any guiding intelligence, voiced in a stanza form of Tennyson's own invention:

> About a stone-cast from the wall
> A sluice with blacken'd waters slept,
> And o'er it many, round and small,
> The cluster'd marish-mosses crept.
> Hard by a poplar shook alway,
> All silver-green with gnarlèd bark:
> For leagues no other tree did mark
> The level waste, the rounding gray.

The uncontrollable shaking of the poplar and the hinted echo of 'nightmarish' in the mosses subtly transfers to the reader's image of the lonely heroine, with her plaintive 'I would that I were dead'. The absence of other trees is reinforced by the utter absence of human sound: the clinking latch, after all, is 'unlifted', and all the sounds in the poem are non-human – the cock, the squeaky doors, the fly, the mouse, the sparrow, and the clock's fatal ticking. This concatenation of the non-human indicates the inevitable impossibility of change for the human protagonist. Much of this is brilliantly conveyed in the opening stanza:

> With blackest moss the flower-plots
>   Were thickly crusted, one and all:
> The rusted nails fell from the knots
>   That held the pear to the gable-wall.
> The broken sheds look'd sad and strange:
>   Unlifted was the clinking latch;
>   Weeded and worn the ancient thatch
> Upon the lonely moated grange.

The past tense of line 2 suggests the immobility of decay, whilst the verb 'look'd' registers an observation of a range of objects from which life and energy have been withdrawn. Nevertheless, as Christopher Ricks has observed, there *is* change in the poem, and this slight but significant sense of movement is embodied in the varying refrain. 'He cometh not', for instance, is finally transmuted to the bleaker 'He will not come'; 'She said, "I am aweary"' shifts to 'She wept, "I am aweary"', and "I would that I were dead"' becomes the more anguished and suicidal '"Oh God, that I were dead"'. This anguish, and the absence of companionship, is beautifully embodied in the shadow of the poplar, the only occupant of the heroine's lonely bed. 'Mariana', with its unformulated plot, is a curiously modern poem. Ricks, in a memorable phrase, speaks of Tennyson's 'art of the penultimate', and this seizes upon the melancholic attraction of situations of postponement for Tennyson. The text is one which, in its onomatopoeic density (Eliot praised the appositeness of the buzzing sound-effect '*sung* in the pane') enacts the meaning created through absence. The landscape of inertia and loss, which will dominate many of the poet's best texts, becomes the objective correlative for a cluster of emotions. What the poem does *not* say is as apt to create or multiply meanings as what it does say. Indeed 'Mariana' is modern in its assumption that loss is fundamentally inscribed in human experience, and that physical absence signals a lack in language itself, a primordial emptiness which can never be transferred into an amplitude.

### 'The Kraken' (1830)

This remarkable exercise in the apocalyptic mode is one of the poet's few really successful attempts at the sonnet form. The Kraken (which

Tennyson had read about in Scott's poetry), 'far beneath the abysmal sea', is impervious to the life of the surface, as 'faintest sunlights flee/ About his shadowy sides'. The life of the submarine depths is rendered with a Shelleyan degree of sensuous curiosity, a sense of fascination and repulsion conjoining in the description of the sponges and the 'Unnumber'd and enormous polypi' whose life is threateningly alien to humanity. Depths of uncharted emotion lie dormant in the text, with its mixed sense of the pleasures and pains of this unplumbed deep. As in some other sea poems, Tennyson here hints at the pleasurable possibilities of drowning, but intermingles a sensuous exactitude which has something of an erotic charge. The erotic and the death instinct coexist in a suspension of human will, and are mirrored in the supple undersea motions enacted in the rhythm. The Kraken itself can only be known or revealed on the Day of Judgement, and visually he is only to be guessed at here. The rhyme-scheme carefully varies the octave and sestet structure, with the final sestet extended to incorporate a return to the dominant words (deep, sleep) of the opening quatrain, a return which also records the weird monotony of the creaturely existence depicted here. The overall effect of the sonnet is of economy of detail and homogeneity of theme in the depiction of a creature pleasingly separated off from the upper world of moral choice and value. Like the Lady of Shalott, the monster wakes up only to die. His monstrous unlikeness to humanity cuts him off from any effect of pantheistic incorporation or sympathy, and he remains irretrievably alien to the narrator and reader. Verbally, the poem appears to recall, in its conjuring up of the 'abysmal sea', Hallam's description, in his essay on sympathy, of the 'abysmal secrets of the personality'. Metaphorically, the poem hints at the secret depths of uncontrolled fantasy life of the author/reader, a life which in its supple indirection and anarchic subterfuge may die when brought into linguistic or poetic form. Read thus, the poem becomes, like 'The Lady of Shalott', a luminous reflection upon the necessary impossibility of poetic utterance, an impossibility nicely registered in George Steiner's remarks upon French Symbolism:

For the writer after Mallarmé language does violence to meaning, flattering, destroying it, as a living thing from the deeps is destroyed when drawn to the daylight and low pressures of the sea surface.[5]

### 'Song: a spirit haunts' (1830)

Of the various songs of this period this one, written at Somersby, is the most successful and potent. There is great subtlety of stress pattern. For example, in line 14 the stress falls upon the 'sick', but the pace of the line is so slow that 'man' is scarcely unstressed either. In the subsequent line, 'My very heart faints and my whole soul grieves', the sound and feel of that opening phrase is like a missed beat of the heart. The overall movement of the verse is downward, from the spirit who earthward 'boweth the heavy stalks', towards the great sunflower hanging over its own grave. The drift of the poem, that is to say, is from the spirit of the opening to the earth of the ending. Both the year and the garden are dying and are metaphorically translated into a typical Victorian death-bed scene. Yet Tennyson artfully creates some pulls against this slide towards inanition. In 'Heavily hangs the hollyhock' the light tripping syllables undermine and modify the gloomy heaviness implicit in the transmutation of 'bowers' to 'boweth'. It is a poem of decay which refers only subliminally to other seasons, yet which endows the moment of decay with a heady and perfumed attraction of its own. An intriguing aspect of the poem is the ambiguous position of the narrative voice, which begins by describing the activities of the gardening spirit in the third person, only later to surprise the reader by intervening in the first person, at 'My very heart faints and my whole soul grieves'. The effect is wayward and complex in its re-creation of the decay and attraction of imagined death. The long-drawn-out lines are effectively juxtaposed with other brief and dramatic lines, such as 'In the walks' and 'And the breath', the reader's mind being impelled onwards in an almost ver-tiginous sway by the sound and rhythm.

# 5. Poems 1832–42

### 'Oenone' (1832; revised 1842)

Oenone, daughter of a river-god, was married to the Trojan prince, Paris. Tennyson makes her a spectator of the judgement whereby Paris gave the apple of discord to Aphrodite, who offered successes in love, rather than to Herè or Pallas, who offered him power and wisdom. This judgement made Aphrodite a friend of Illion (Troy), and the others its enemies. As the successful lover of Helen, Paris deserted Oenone.

Tennyson began this poem in the French Pyrenees at a time when he may himself have faced something akin to the choice presented to Paris, a choice between a life devoted to the senses, and the world of the intellect which lay behind him at Cambridge. 'Oenone' is a somewhat hybrid work, since it attempts to combine the lament of the heroine, a wood-nymph, with the more ethical questions involved in the judgement of Paris. Paris's preference for beauty and love as against power and wisdom raises in acute form the question which was to motivate many of Tennyson's poems – what *is* the supreme good in human life? For the Victorian reading public, it may have seemed that the young poet sounded a resonant chord in his rehearsal of the current debate about the alternatives proffered by the Utilitarians, the Christian Humanists, and the Romantic poets. Herè, in offering the gift of power as the sole means of making Paris one of the gods, specifically associates her gift with the philosophy of Epicurus, a philosophy strikingly close to the Utilitarian creed espoused by Mill and Bentham.

She declares that power is the hidden motivation behind all human acts, and implies that through its use the face of nature itself may be transformed. To this curiously mid-Victorian sentiment, Pallas makes angry rebuttal:

> 'Self-reverence, self-knowledge, self-control,
> These three alone lead life to sovereign power.
> Yet not for power (power of herself
> Would come uncall'd for) but to live by law,
> Acting the law we live by without fear;
> And, because right is right, to follow right
> Were wisdom in the scorn of consequence.'

Pallas here focuses the reader's attention upon the most knotty issue between the Utilitarians and the Christian Humanists, by her implication that values are absolute, not relative. Goodness, that is to say, is achieved not by a human working upon the face of nature, but by transforming ourselves. It is through renunciation, and submission of the will to eternal law, that we achieve real power and freedom, the freedom of self-control. Hearing this solemn message, Oenone cries 'O Paris,/ Give it to Pallas', but instead Paris 'ponders' the dichotomies presented. Aphrodite seductively approaches Paris so that her naked beauty will make its full impact upon him, and, with a 'subtle smile . . . The herald of her triumph', whispers into his ear, '"I promise thee/ The fairest and most loving wife in Greece"', after which she laughs. This uncanny laughter arises not only out of the contemplation of the weakness of men and mortals, but out of foreknowledge of the future destruction brought on by the Trojan wars: there is a commingled sense of attraction to the erotic and to violence which would be crystallized into the terrible power of Yeats's 'Leda and the Swan'. Aphrodite possesses the 'subtle' smile of the literary *femme fatale* who lures men to their destruction, and the upshot is a predictable melting of Paris into sexual desire. Carnal love of this kind, the poem is suggesting, is deathly in its impact, and Pallas's instruction is good and true. Yet with her 'snow-cold breast' Pallas is not an attractive figure, and it is often hard to see why Oenone, as a passionate wood-nymph, would choose to side with her. In a passage added in 1842 Oenone seeks out the figure of Discord to revile her for her impact upon human life, and Paris recognizes that the inscription, 'for the fairest', applies not to either of the conflicting goddesses but to Oenone herself. The violation of Oenone is suggested symbolically by the parallel invasion of nature when the pines are cut down and the bower ruined:

> 'They came, they cut away my tallest pines,
> My tall dark pines, that plumed the craggy ledge
> High over the blue gorge, and all between
> The snowy peak and snow-white cataract
> Foster'd the callow eaglet'

Oenone is evidently associated with the soft mist in the valley which 'slopes athwart the glen,/ Puts forth an arm, creeps from pine to pine', and this enveloping mist serves to unify an otherwise disparate text. Unlike other Tennysonian heroines, Oenone does not resign herself to passive suffering but emerges from the vale to pronounce words of doom on the evil city of Troy:

> 'I will rise and go
> Down into Troy, and ere the stars come forth
> Talk with the wild Cassandra, for she says
> A fire dances before her, and a sound
> Rings ever in her ears of armèd men.
> What this may be I know not, but I know
> That, wheresoe'er I am by night and day,
> All earth and air seem only burning fire.'

Overall, Tennyson attempts in 'Oenone' a complexity of viewpoint which he is not able to sustain, and the result is a text of productive confusion. Some characteristic sound effects which depend largely upon the successful deployment of liquid consonantal sounds are awkwardly juxtaposed with much sententious public moralizing. The delicacy of the opening lines, conjuring up the ambience of the deserted nymph, is not successfully sustained. but there are lines which serve to create a potently eroticized landscape, and Ricks is just in speaking of a 'healthy furtiveness' in Tennyson's effects here. In its fiery close the poem predicts not only the destruction of Troy but Oenone's own funeral pyre, to which she will ascend in the later 'The Death of Oenone'. It is, however, the lusciously ripe evocation of the primal valley which the reader of 'Oenone' carries away when the moral argument is discarded:

> There lies a vale in Ida, lovelier
> Than all the valleys of Ionian hills.
> The swimming vapour slopes athwart the glen,
> Puts forth an arm, and creeps from pine to pine,
> And loiters, slowly drawn. On either hand
> The lawns and meadow-ledges midway down
> Hang rich in flowers, and far below them roars
> The long brook falling thro' the clov'n ravine
> In cataract after cataract to the sea.

'Oenone' debates the notion of truth within its textuality, and the forms which truth appears to take are reflected and created through different and contradictory patterns of discourse. Against the densely figural language of this opening, which claims to describe and re-create the natural environment, may be juxtaposed a type of philosophical discourse:

> 'Still she spake on and still she spake of power,
> "Which in all action is the end of all;
> Power fitted to the season; wisdom-bred
> And throned of wisdom ..."'

That such language may lay claim to a higher 'truth' is allowed but simultaneously challenged by the poem, which seeks to lay bare the will to power vested in such language and such claims to have access to an unchanging truth. The highly figural language of Oenone's vision, that is to say, may be no more 'poetic' in its relation to a supposed truth-content than the apparently more rational discourse of the goddess. Philosophy seeks to impose a hierarchy of discourse which prioritizes clear and rational statement; yet such statement is itself totally immersed in, and unconscious of, figural devices. The 'truths' delivered by such language may, therefore, be no more or less fictional than the truths of poetry, and far less potent in their working upon the reader. 'Oenone' may thus productively be read as an exemplification of Paul de Man's claim that 'philosophy turns out to be an endless reflection on its own destruction at the hands of literature'. The poem, in other words, whilst overtly supporting the truth claims of rationality and thought, implicitly unravels such claims. It is as though Tennyson, in endorsing the superior claims of reason and philosophy, unconsciously endows the literary and imaginative with rhetorical supremacy in a field of discourse dominated by and created through metaphoric effect. Oenone's repeated refrain works to create an effect of monotony which expresses her baffled frustrations. The lament of the poem begins in the noontide heat, and ends at sunset as she foresees her own death. Most interestingly, perhaps, 'Oenone' reveals in its fecund Arcadian landscapes a hidden potential for betrayal and death which will erupt in the Trojan wars.

## 'The Lady of Shalott' (1832; revised version 1842)

Looking back upon the composition of this remarkable poem, Tennyson could not later in his life recall whether he had read of Malory's 'Lily maid of Astolat'. His immediate source, the medieval Italian romance of the *Donna di Scalotta*, is another Arthurian variant telling how a damsel dies for love of Lancelot du Lac, but there is no web, mirror or island in that version. The damsels who haunt Tennyson's juvenilia – Claribel, Lilian, Isabel and Mariana – indicated his interest in the emblematic lady who appears first in Romantic poetry, and would memorably inhabit so many Pre-Raphaelite paintings. The Lady of Shalott, portrayed later by Holman Hunt, Millais and Rossetti, became the type of the enclosed female, locked in contemplation. It was to be a seminal poem for the age, touching, perhaps unwittingly, on the vexed question of the position and rights of women, and referring allegorically to the nature and dangers of the creative imagination. The way in which 'The Lady of

Shalott' entered the imagination of the reading public is nicely registered by Birkin's complaint to Ursula in D. H. Lawrence's *Women in Love*, written during the Great War:

'It's all that Lady of Shalott business,' he said ... 'You've got that mirror, your own fixed will, your immortal understanding, your own tight conscious world, and there is nothing beyond it. There, in the mirror, you must have everything.'

The figure of the secluded lady looking out upon a male world of action became archetypal in the Victorian novel, where Tennyson's poem surfaces repeatedly as an intertext.[6]

The stanza form is strict and demanding: the first quatrain has four rhymes, the second quatrain three, and each verse is rounded off with a refrain:

> On either side the river lie
> Long fields of barley and of rye,
> That clothe the wold and meet the sky;
> And thro' the field the road runs by
>     To many-tower'd Camelot;
> And up and down the people go,
> Gazing where the lilies blow
> Round an island there below,
>     The island of Shalott.

In the second stanza Tennyson shifts to a feminine rhyme and moves from the tripping rhythm of 'Willows whiten, aspens quiver' to the slow, drawn-out rhythm of 'Four gray walls, and four gray towers'. The verse movement proposes a dramatic polarity between Shalott and Camelot which will be enhanced in the poem. By placing the first two parts in the present tense, and the second two in the past, the poet increases the sense of disruption and disturbance to the pleasant order of the castle, a disruption which the reader hears in the alliterative 'b's' of Lancelot's arrival:

> A bow-shot from her bower-eaves,
> He rode between the barley-sheaves,
> The sun came dazzling thro' the leaves,
> And flamed upon the brazen greaves
>     Of bold Sir Lancelot.

Each of the four parts ends with speech: the reaper's whispered gossip, the lady's complaint, her acknowledgement of the curse, and Lancelot's musing upon her face. It seems to be the sight of the two young lovers 'lately wed' which motivates her cry, and this discontent is focused upon the dazzling sight of Lancelot:

> All in the blue unclouded weather
> Thick-jewell'd shone the saddle-leather,
> The helmet and the helmet-feather
> Burn'd like one burning flame together,
>    As he rode down to Camelot.

The knight appears both in direct reflection in the lady's mirror, which she uses for her embroidery, and in indirect reflection from the surface of the river:

> From the bank and from the river
> He flash'd into the crystal mirror,
> 'Tirra lirra,' by the river
>    Sang Sir Lancelot.

The rhyme 'river/river', as the poet pointed out, represents and mimics that reflectiveness of surfaces, and the poem has often been read as a statement about the nature of art which derives some of its potency from Plato's myth of the cave. Plato's argument that art is a reflection of a reality which is itself a reflection of an ideal world may go some way to explaining the dangers of the lady's act in deserting the reflexive mirror for a wider 'reality', and the poem clearly feeds upon Tennyson's own anxieties about the relationship between his art and society at large. The poet is reported to have said of his lady, 'the new-born love for something, for some one in the wide world from which she has been so long secluded, takes her out of the region of shadows into that of reality'.

The act of the female looking in the mirror, often a crucial scene in Victorian art and literature, indicates a lack of differentiation between a 'self' and an 'other'. There is, in the poem, a sense of optical repetition, of Lancelot's 'double' reflected and refracted from both river and mirror, so that the eye of the lady must in a sense generate both his identity and the forms of nature which she loves to 'see'. There is a highly erotic feeling about the use of the mirror, which goes with the conjunction of the sun with Lancelot, and the way light will, as it were, play upon the female shape in the mirror. Tennyson gives the reader a highly suggestive concatenation of light, water and mirror: through the reflection in the mirror the 'self' comes into being, but reflection of light also disrupts and breaks that existence, with disastrous results for the lady. The stasis of the mirror is placed against the motion of the river, the whole knit, like her 'web', into a chain of metaphorical transformations. In the

Freudian mirror-phase the infant is fixed, constrained within representation, and this may be contrasted with the flow of the maternal milk. Whilst the mirror represents and creates fixed identity, the locking away of the 'self' of the lady, the river represents the primordial life-flow prior to the construction of the self. The final transformation, in which Lancelot expresses our readerly sense of mystery and wonderment in a brilliant misreading of the lady's dead physiognomy, possesses supreme fitness, since it touches both upon the Arthurian matter of his affair with Guinevere, and upon the tragic plight of the artist who is in and yet not of this world.

Tennyson's story subliminally refers to the legend about a fairy who falls in love with a mortal. In claiming him for herself, she dies. The lady is an elusive, withdrawn figure somewhat akin to Shelley's Witch of Atlas. Lancelot, in contrast, is visualized in dazzling light and noise, as if he were the sun deity to her moon goddess. The poem arranges its meanings through a hierarchy of gender polarities in which 'male' is action and aggression and 'female' withdrawal and inactivity.

The image of burning is primarily sexual, and hints also at the destructive effects of passion:

> The helmet and the helmet-feather
> Burn'd like one burning flame together,
>    As he rode down to Camelot.

By violating the 'curse' the lady becomes subject to time, destruction and decay:

> Out flew the web and floated wide;
> The mirror crack'd from side to side;
> 'The curse is come upon me,' cried
>    The Lady of Shalott.

Within her solitary tower world, shadows participate, albeit vicariously, in the movement and activity of life, the barges, the shallops in the river, the abbot, the knights, the damsels, the shepherd, and the wedding and funeral processions. Her action transforms her into the type of the dying swan, whose final life-force is concentrated in its song. The lady has earlier sung a different song, which is overheard by the reapers, but whereas both her songs attempt to encapsulate life in art forms, the 'Tirra lirra' of Lancelot is a meaningless outpouring of vital energy against which the reader balances the 'carol, mournful, holy,/ Chanted loudly, chanted lowly' of the darkening conclusion.

The lady does not live in the world, but weaves her web from a reflection. Her name and 'Camelot' are the refrain words, but seemingly cannot be fully integrated with each other. It is as if the lady possesses no real sense of identity apart from what is seen in the mirror. When she decides she is 'sick of shadows' she inscribes the name 'The Lady of Shalott' on the prow of the boat, asserting her selfhood in a doomed attempt to enter into the social conviviality represented by Camelot. In this way the poem demonstrates how significant language may be in bringing with it a sense of identity, an identity fatally attractive to the lady, as the original conclusion crudely revealed:

> There lay a parchment on her breast,
> That puzzled more than all the rest,
> The wellfed wits at Camelot.
> 'The web was woven curiously
> The charm is broken utterly,
> Draw near and fear not – this is I,
> The Lady of Shalott.'

The poem may be read as a parodic intertext of the medieval cult of courtly love, wherein the woman is exalted (literally and metaphorically) into the place where her inaccessibility stands as a substitute for male lack. Woman, in the mythical figure, represents difference and loss. The 'phallic' nature of Lancelot defines the lady by that which she does not possess, so that she becomes, as classically she is in so many Pre-Raphaelite images of her, a fantasy object, an 'Other' which threatens and disrupts phallic knowledge and authority and so must be destroyed. 'The Lady of Shalott' reverses the archetypal Victorian patterning in which the male glance centres erotically upon the female, and this may be the reason for the lady's sufferings. The text, that is, produces the image of woman, but simultaneously insists that that image is unknowable – as Lancelot's final words, an act of misinterpretation, indicate to the reader. Tennyson here creates a potent fantasy of exhibitionism and secrecy in which the erotic life of the heroine is curiously displaced into the features of the landscape.

In one of the most interesting recent readings of the poem, Geoffrey Hartman[7] sees it as pondering the difficulties of absolute knowledge or possession. To know, he argues, 'means a desire to be defined totally: marked or named once and for all, fixed on by a word, and so – paradoxically – made indifferent':

'I am half sick of shadows', says the Lady of Shalott, and turns from her mirror to the reality of advent. She did not know that by her avertedness, by staying within representation, she had postponed death.

49

The sense of an ultimate reality is placed within the aesthetic object – poem, embroidery – itself. Art, Hartman says, 'is a mirror language' which burns out 'the desire for self-definition, fullness of grace, presence; simply to expose the desire to own one's own name, to inhabit it numinously in the form of "proper" noun, words, or the signatory act each poem aspires to be'. The poem, in such a reading, transcends that loss, absence which Tennyson so deeply feared; as Hartman suggests:

Poem and lady remain immaculate though web, mirror, or spell may break. Such impossibility is perhaps part of the infection, an unresolved narcissism of festering lily or psyche.

Artistic withdrawal is, in this text, neither applauded nor condemned. The self is immured in its own consciousness, but drawn outwards by the powers of sexual attraction and natural beauty, into an act of self-annihilation. The polarity established between stasis and dynamism is crucial to the meanings of the poem, meanings which resound and multiply like the images in the lady's mirror.

## 'The Lotos-Eaters' (1832; revised 1842)

Tennyson calls up memories of Greek classical myth in this Spenserian experiment in order to evoke a contrast between a past world of heroic male action and the golden retreat of the island which offered rest to the sailors of Odysseus. The morality is cunningly embedded in the text, so that unlike 'Oenone', there is here a degree of productive ambiguity for the readerly mind to tease away at. Once the mariners have eaten of the lotus fruit, they lapse into a somnambulistic trance, and at the opening of the poem their idle resignation is experienced as a form of resistance to the active order of their commander:

> 'Courage!' he said, and pointed toward the land,
> 'This mounting wave will roll us shore-ward soon.'
> In the afternoon they came unto a land
> In which it seemèd always afternoon.
> All round the coast the languid air did swoon,
> Breathing like one that hath a weary dream.
> Full-faced above the valley stood the moon;
> And like a downward smoke, the slender stream
> Along the cliff to fall and pause and fall did seem.

The final line, depicting the waterfall, has been aptly characterized as 'the slowest in English literature'. The stanza, in its vigorous opening, falls away into the stillness and attractive languor of inactivity, a languor nicely marked, as Tennyson himself observed, by the laziness of the 'land/land' rhyme substitute. The stanza is Spenserian, with its nine lines elongated to produce both 'a free lyricism and a menacing pressure' (Ricks). The opening stanzas set the scene for what appears to be a poem of seduction, dealing, like *Antony and Cleopatra*, with an abundant life which may also bring death in its train. The 'land of streams' is enervating and lifeless, in a climate where 'it seemèd always afternoon'. All things 'ripen towards the grave/ In silence'. The Choric Song picks up a different verse movement, in which descriptions of the island alternate with reflections upon the mariners' drugged state. Within the song, a note of responsibility is sounded, only to be lost again. The rhythm here is certainly more tense:

> Is there confusion in the little isle?
> Let what is broken so remain.
> The Gods are hard to reconcile:
> 'Tis hard to settle order once again.
> There *is* confusion worse than death,
> Trouble on trouble, pain on pain,
> Long labour unto agèd breath,
> Sore task to hearts worn out by many wars
> And eyes grown dim with gazing on the pilot-stars.

The appeal throughout the text is for a kind of paradisal life freed from effort, so that the sailors may be seen as early 'drop-outs', their Choric Song an affirmation of their will-less passivity. A glance at Homer reminds us that the vigorous attitude of the opening finally prevailed, but that only Odysseus himself will survive their further wanderings. *The Odyssey*, IX, tells us:

And whosoever of them ate the honey-sweet fruit of the lotus, had no longer any wish to return, but there they were fain to abide among the lotus-eaters, feeding on the lotus, and forgetful of their homeward ways. These men, therefore, I brought back perforce to the ships, weeping.

The poem is, however, more than a brilliant technical exercise inspired by Homer. The island is envisaged as a place outside the reach of European merchant capital, and the attitude into which the mariners fall is plainly antithetical to the Smilesian doctrine of self-help which had fuelled the industrial revolution. If we follow Alan Sinfield's suggestion,[8] the poem can also be read as a meditation upon the marginality of poetry itself within the utilitarian hegemony of the period. Tennyson preserves a critical balance between sympathy and judgement in the reader. It is difficult to resist the appeal voiced in the poem to a life of indolent ease and delight in the senses; the world of change is rejected for a world of sameness, but a sameness which promises ecstasy. The lotus seems curiously to allow complete self-absorption, and also communality, as the poem suggests in 'The flower ripens in its place,/ Ripens and fades, and falls, and hath no toil,/ Fast-rooted in the fruitful soil'. The final line of the poem expresses rather more than an appeal to the 'brother mariners': it is a direct appeal to the reader, an appeal which we can neither wholly embrace nor, such is the subtlety of the art, reject.

### 'Ulysses' (1842)

Ulysses is about to leave his island kingdom of Ithaca to his prudent and dutiful son Telemachus and set out on a great adventure which may reunite him with his dead companion of the Trojan wars, Achilles. In this fine monologue Tennyson meditates creatively upon the death of Hallam. Indeed, the poem was completed within three weeks of Tennyson hearing the fatal news. The poet claimed that the chief model for his poem was not the Homeric protagonist but rather Dante's Ulisse, a mighty sinner with an insatiable thirst for knowledge and experience. 'Ulysses' may be read on one level as expression of the triumph of the will, but it is a more complex work than such a description allows for. Whilst Ulysses speaks of noble work and demonstrates that Ithaca requires such Carlylean virtues, he is essentially passive and has left the cares of office to Telemachus. Although he claims that he is seeking knowledge, the reader may reflect that he seeks oblivion through activity. Once again, the poem precariously balances the claims of action and escape. Ulysses faces the alternatives of a useful life, tending to the well-. being of his people:

> . . . by slow prudence to make mild
> A rugged people, and thro' soft degrees
> Subdue them to the useful and the good.

or a life of travel and the exotic, 'To follow knowledge like a sinking star,/ Beyond the utmost bound of human thought'. The poem falls into four sub-sections, two declaring nobility of aim and two running counter to this nobility. The first movement (11.1–5) is restless and even bitter in its rejection of domesticity: diction and rhythm are harsh and explosive, notably in the undermining of traditional views of Penelope as the ideal wife. Home appears unattractive and mean. The second movement (11.6–

32) contrasts this sense of dissatisfaction with a gloriously remembered and celebrated past, the language moulding itself into a positively Homeric resonance and re-enactment of the deeds of heroism. But the subversive undercurrent hinted at in Ulysses' somewhat indiscriminate attitude to experience, in drinking life 'to the lees', erupts into the third movement (11.33–43), where the heroic speaker again recalls the listener to the Ithaca he seems to despise. The rhythm here is flat, the energy dissipated into a somewhat bored acceptance of the necessity of those civic virtues to which Ulysses himself can never aspire, and this complex of ideas is concentrated in the description of the role of his son Telemachus:

> Well-loved of me, discerning to fulfil
> This labour, by slow prudence to make mild
> A rugged people, and thro' soft degrees
> Subdue them to the useful and the good.
> Most blameless is he, centred in the sphere
> Of common duties, decent not to fail
> In offices of tenderness, and pay
> Meet adoration to my household gods,
>     When I am gone.

In the final peroration (11.47–70) Tennyson seeks to resolve, through grandeur of language and exercise of poetic decorum, the tensions set up in his monologue. Yet the declarative utterance and devil-may-care mood is subtly undercut by the melancholy sound of the verse which mimetically acts out a very different mood:

> The lights begin to twinkle from the rocks:
> The long day wanes: the slow moon climbs: the deep
> Moans round with many voices. Come, my friends,
> 'Tis not too late to seek a newer world.

There is perhaps a muffled note of hysteria in 'Come, my friends . . .', a note which is not altogether lost in the Churchillian gestures of the ending.

'Ulysses' is a poem which generates meaning by postulating an Ithaca which represents limitation of human action. The vocabulary associated with Ulysses' home – 'idle', 'still', 'barren', 'savage' – suggests sterility and stagnation. For the hero 'all experience is an arch wherethro'/ Gleams that untravell'd world', and the final night voyage, like the one projected in D. H. Lawrence's 'Ship of Death', is towards the unknown region, the beyond. Death is thus the final adventure which Ulysses imagines for himself, and his resounding 'To strive, to seek, to find, and not to yield' carries dangerous echoes of the Satanic 'courage never to submit or yield' of Milton's *Paradise Lost*. Speaking later about *In Memoriam*, Tennyson asserted: 'There is more about myself in "Ulysses", which was written under the sense of loss and that all had gone by, but that still life must be fought out to the end.' Ricks is perhaps just in detecting in the poem a 'plumped amplitude' of utterance, and in discerning in the picturing of the heroic man of action a Tennysonian undertone of ennui and aimlessness. If Tennyson's characters notably seek rest through oblivion, 'Ulysses' brilliantly dramatizes that search by its adoption of a cult of manly activity and adventure wholly characteristic of its period. Indeed, an early reader of the poem claimed that Ulysses 'intends to roam, but stands for ever a listless and melancholy figure on the shore'. There is a powerful longing in the poem to be able to believe that life consists not only of the past but also of a future, but that future is always hedged about in the linguistic forms of the text: the future is both deeply desired and unimaginable.

The complexities of interpretation provoked by 'Ulysses' are nicely illuminated in a critical exchange published in a useful collection of essays on the poet.[9] In the view of E. J. Chiasson, 'Ulysses' takes its place in the Tennysonian canon as one of many expressions 'of Tennyson's conviction that religious faith is mandatory for . . . the needs of life'. Countering the view that Hallam's death provides the right context for interpretation of the poem, Chiasson argues that the text expounds the position that 'life without faith leads to personal and social dislocation'. *In Memoriam*, 34, expresses the view that life without a sense of immortality is a monstrous notion, and Chiasson reads the dramatic monologue in the light of this postulate. Analysing the second movement of the poem Chiasson discerns a lack of religious insight: 'Drinking life to the lees, drinking delight of battle with his peers, following knowledge like a sinking star – all render [Ulysses] abundantly lyrical.' There is, in other words, no indication that richness and multiplicity of experience endow Ulysses with wisdom and insight. The grudging respect for Telemachus takes its place within this reading: the hero is content to let his son get on with the duties of religious observance, whilst he strives in company either with, or against, the gods. Thus the comforting reassurance in the final section, that perhaps he and his men will reach the Happy Isles, is 'tonally indifferent'. Ulysses, that is to say, is himself indifferent and impervious to questions of immortality; he is, rather, a spokesman for a kind of 'jovial agnosticism' which would characterize the later Victorian period. W. W. Robson, by contrast, salutes the Carlylean seriousness he discerns in the poem, but argues that, in this text, the poet is evidently *not* 'at one with an aspiration of his age'. Tennyson's speaker is a 'self-conscious poet', to the extent that there is 'no discrepancy between the strenuousness aspired to, and the medium in which the aspiration is expressed'. The relationship between the poet and his public is thus nakedly exposed in all its contradictions here: the tensions between Tennyson 'the responsible social being' and Tennyson 'the depressed private poet' work to create an ambiguous poetic rhetoric, to the extent, Robson argues, that 'it often looks as if Tennyson the moralist and Tennyson the artist are functioning on entirely separate planes'. In this reading, therefore, 'Ulysses' is a seminally split text which portends, despite or because of its powerful resonance and unity, the breakdown of the relationship between Tennyson's art and his social conscience, a breakdown which Robson detects in such later work as 'Locksley Hall Sixty Years After'.

'Ulysses' may be read as a poem about the will: all is finally transmuted and absorbed into the hero's own ego. He has rejected the values of community and relationship, so that the final lines both exhilarate and sadden the reader.

### 'St Simeon Stylites' (1842)

Simeon was a fifth-century hermit, reputed to have spent thirty years on top of a pillar sixty feet high. His surname is the Greek for 'pillar'. Escapism is firmly rejected here in one of Tennyson's favourite poems, and one of his earliest experiments in the form of the dramatic monologue. The monologue form enabled the poet to express an imagined other life, to preserve a tension between the voice of the speaker and the overarching voice of the poet himself. Tennyson places his saint, the Eastern ascetic, upon a pillar forty cubits high, but makes the figure prey to some sense of panic about his own salvation. It would appear that the poem embedded a parodic allusion to the Reverend Charles Simeon, the leading Cambridge Evangelical of Tennyson's day, who annoyed many students by the strictness of his view of the religious life. The saint here speaks in tones of deep humility which, like those of Eliot's Becket, denote an overweening spiritual pride. Simeon insists upon his sinfulness, whilst believing himself elevated morally, spiritually (and physically) above his fellow men:

> Altho' I be the basest of mankind,
> From scalp to sole one slough and crust of sin,

55

> Unfit for earth, unfit for heaven, scarce meet
> For troops of devils, mad with blasphemy,
> I will not cease to grasp the hope I hold
> Of saintdom,

The dying Simeon occasionally confuses himself with his Saviour, and makes vaunt of the appalling sufferings to which he has subjected himself:

> . . . half deaf I am,
> So that I scarce can hear the people hum
> About the column's base, and almost blind,
> And scarce can recognise the fields I know;
> And both my thighs are rotted with the dew;

Simeon's vaunted sins, and his self-inflicted punishment, are his path to glory:

> . . . On the coals I lay,
> A vessel full of sin: all hell beneath
> Made me boil over. Devils pluck'd my sleeve,

Simeon's passivity in suffering is neatly juxtaposed with his highly active mental life. From the 'grasp' at the hope of sainthood in line five, to the 'clutch' at the crown sixteen lines from the end, Simeon is always defined by his lust for sanctity, and there is a veritable hint of the grotesque in the catalogue of his sufferings. As the saint's urgent claim to merit is partly built upon self-deception, so is the confirmation of his sanctity. The 'proof' of his fitness for heaven is the cry of the populace: ''Tis their own doing; this is none of mine;/ Lay it not on me'. The poem is more complex than this suggests, touching, as does T. S. Eliot's *Murder in the Cathedral*, upon the tissue of worthy and unworthy motivations inevitably involved in cases of martyrdom. As one commentator judiciously remarks, 'Simeon is incapable, at this stage of his life, of discerning the contradiction inherent in conscious, premeditated martyrdom'. The poem ends prior to Simeon's death. He asks for the sacrament:

> For by the warning of the Holy Ghost,
> I prophesy that I shall die tonight,
> A quarter before twelve.

This is, therefore, another of Tennyson's 'poems of the penultimate', balanced between the uncertainty of Simeon's present state and the genuine martyrdom of which the reader is already apprised. It is a text which presents and enacts a monstrous parody of the aims and ideals of Christianity, the energy of the utterance going some way towards making the reader complicit in Simeon's suffering and claims. The terrible absurdity and necessity of suffering which the poem insists upon may also be a distinguishing mark of Christianity itself, and the reader is left to ponder the case of Simeon as a not wholly untypical case of the religious life.

The text circles warily around the term 'saint', and its reiterated presence both defines and empties the term of meaning. The cunning of the dramatic monologue allows a doubt as to whether Simeon can indeed claim sanctity for himself. The crucial line, 'And lower voices saint me from above' creates a suggestive ambivalence through the antithesis of 'lower' and 'above': the reader (and the poet) may finally remain baffled at the symptoms of martyrdom here presented.

### 'Tithonus' (1833; published 1860)

Tithonus was loved by Aurora, the goddess of the dawn, who gave him immortality but omitted also to give him eternal youth. Although Tennyson did not publish this poem until 1860, at the insistence of Thackeray, 'Tithon', the original rather shorter poem, dates from the period immediately following Hallam's death. Withered in his extreme old age, like Eliot's Gerontion, Tithonus finds marriage no longer a blessing. Below the surface of this lament about the fading of youth, there lurks a sense of foreboding about a possible loss of the poet's own creative power:

> Ay me! ay me! with what another heart
> In days far-off, and with what other eyes
> I used to watch – if I be he that watch'd –
> The lucid outline forming round thee; saw
> The dim curls kindle into sunny rings;
> Changed with thy mystic change, and felt my blood
> Glow with the glow that slowly crimson'd all
> Thy presence and thy portals,

Tithonus can now discover within himself no responsive fervour:

> Coldly thy rosy shadows bathe me, cold
> Are all thy lights, and cold my wrinkled feet
> Upon thy glimmering thresholds,

With the death of his beloved Hallam, the poet had lost the active joy in the imagination which had marked his early work. In his youth, kissed by the dawn, Tithonus 'could hear the lips that kiss'd/ Whispering I knew not what of wild and sweet'. In the revised text, Tennyson omitted Tithonus's threat to bring death itself into the halls of Aurora. This emendation makes it clear that the gift of immortality, like the gift of poetry, cannot be undone. The speaker lives a paradoxically unnatural life within the beauty of nature, and the opening of the poem memorably conjures up the natural cycle to which the hero can now never return – it is that which is always already lost:

> The woods decay, the woods decay and fall,
> The vapours weep their burthen to the ground,
> Man comes and tills the field and lies beneath,
> And after many a summer dies the swan.
> Me only cruel immortality
> Consumes: I wither slowly in thine arms,
> Here at the quiet limit of the world,
> A white-haired shadow roaming like a dream
> The ever-silent spaces of the East,
> Far-folded mists, and gleaming halls of morn.

The stately rhythm with its elegiac sound is disturbed by the inversion in line 5, and the steely suggestion of cruelty in prolonged consumption. Tithonus is thus marginalized by his immortality, torn between the antithetical images of light and dark which energize the poem. The monologue is imagined as being spoken at the moment of dawn, the slowly pacing rhythm enacting the gradual spread of light. The almost grotesque love scene portrays the wasted old man's body in the arms of the goddess:

> Can thy love
> Thy beauty, make amends, tho' even now,
> Close over us, the silver star, thy guide,
> Shines in those tremulous eyes that fill with tears
> To hear me?

The silver star, close at hand and distant, both confirms and threatens.

At the close of his monologue, Tithonus, trying to look towards death, can still recall the past:

> Yet hold me not for ever in thine East:
> How can my nature longer mix with thine?
> Coldly thy rosy shadows bathe me, cold
> Are all thy lights, and cold my wrinkled feet
> Upon thy glimmering thresholds, when the steam

Floats up from those dim fields about the homes
Of happy men that have the power to die,
And grassy barrows of the happier dead.

Henry James characterized the ending as 'poised and stationary', and argued that the 'immobility' defeated the 'dramatic intention'. Such a 'defeat' is always likely in Tennyson, and it seems clear that the poem expresses the shocked realization of a long and meaningless future which came upon Tennyson at the news of Hallam's death. Ricks goes so far as to call the poem Tennyson's 'subtlest and most beautiful exploration of the impulse to suicide', and draws attention to the effect of silence in the poem. In the past, it seems, speech existed, but the only direct speech in the poem is the recall of the fatal request, 'Give me immortality'. The poet's note to this poem, which was designed as a pendant to 'Ulysses', rather grimly undercuts its noble effects. Tithonus, we are told, 'grew old and infirm, and as he could not die, according to the legend, was turned into a grasshopper'.

In a productive reading of the poem, Alan Sinfield suggests that the shadowiness of the 'I' here creates a doubt 'about whether there is a human subject there at all'. The underlying notion of continuance, which is vital to subjectivity, is questioned: 'with what other eyes/ I used to watch – if I be he that watch'd'. The description of the dawn, 'Thy cheek begins to redden thro' the gloom . . .', may be read, Sinfield urges, either as the projection of human feeling on to nature or as the construction of the subject by the world outside. Immortality equals coldness and silence, whilst paradoxically, warmth and immediacy are concomitants of death. In evading the Romantic 'I' through the form of the monologue, Tithonus becomes, in this reading of the text, 'a figure of the poet', marginalized and cut off from the 'kindly race of men'.

The woods, the husbandman and the swan are all subject to the ageing process; they 'ripen towards the grave'. Tithonus has sought to stave off the fate of the 'kindly race of men', and the natural cycle which he evades is illustrated by the role ascribed to Eos. She has attained eternal youth, but only because she submits to the laws of nature, dying each day to awaken the next morning. 'Tithonus' is perhaps not finally a poem of suicide or escape, since the speaker asks, albeit plaintively, to be incorporated within the commonality of all created life.

### 'Morte d'Arthur' (1842)

Tennyson composed the poem, prompted again by the death of Hallam, during 1833–4; he created a framing poem called 'The Epic' around

1839, and published it entire in 1842. It was later to be incorporated into *Idylls of the King*. The poem takes its situation from Malory's claim that King Arthur is not dead, 'but by the will of our Lord in another place', a place whence 'men say he will come again'. The strange and contested disappearance of the vanquished king gives the poet a fine objective correlative for his grief, and in the figure of Bedivere and his equivocations over the dazzling sword, Excalibur, we may discern the character of the poet and his feelings about his art. Although Bedivere is dazzled by the beauty of the sword, with its 'Myriads of topaz-lights, and jacinth-work/ Of subtlest jewellery', he finally adheres to Arthur's sombre wishes and returns it to the Lady of the Lake. The implication here may be of a gradual subduing of the verbal dexterity and musical incantation of the early verse into a more sober mode of utterance.

Arthur is conceived as one who has brought order into being. It is through the power of Excalibur that Arthur forged the Round Table, and it is back to the mysterious sources represented by the Lady of the Lake that the sword must be hurled, despite Bedivere's wish that it might be preserved for posterity:

> . . . were this kept,
> Stored in some treasure-house of mighty kings,
> Some one might show it at a joust of arms,
> Saying, 'King Arthur's sword, Excalibur,
> Wrought by the lonely maiden of the Lake.'

The landscape of the action is brilliantly re-created in all its barren splendour, and when the three queens send up their lamentation it is 'like a wind, that shrills/ All night in a waste land, where no one comes,/ Or hath come, since the making of the world'. Although Arthur's mind is 'clouded with a doubt', he believes he is going:

> To the island-valley of Avilion;
> Where falls not hail, or rain, or any snow,
> Nor ever wind blows loudly; but it lies
> Deep meadow'd, happy, fair with orchard-lawns
> And bowery hollows crown'd with summer sea,

Avalon is thus imaged here as a 'feminine' place in contrast to the harshly 'masculine' qualities of the 'dark strait of barren land' to which Arthur retreats after the last battle in the west, with its 'zig-zag paths, and juts of pointed rock'. The organizing principle of the poem is one of recurrence within an endless cycle of birth, death and rebirth, as Arthur instructs his grieving follower:

'The old order changeth, yielding place to new,
    And God Fulfils Himself in many ways,
    Lest one good custom should corrupt the world.'

The strait of barren land set between ocean and lake seems an apt symbol of man's life, poised between the great unknown territories of birth and death. The emphasis upon the number three – the three attempts of Sir Bedivere, three wavings of the sword, and the three queens – may be emblematic of the underlying cycle of birth, death and rebirth upon which the poem is posited.

Bedivere gradually learns to view experience more spiritually, and it is essentially his learning experience that is at the heart of the poem. When he can attain to a greater insight, he is rewarded by a vision in which the sword dazzlingly impersonates the effects of the aurora borealis:

            . . . The great brand
    Made lightnings in the splendour of the moon,
    And flashing round and round, and whirl'd in an arch,
    Shot like a streamer of the northern morn,
    Seen where the moving isles of winter shock
    By night, with noises of the northern sea.

The 'moon/morn' half-rhyme here serves nicely to create the mysterious resonance of Bedivere's vision, a vision which occurs as part of a gradual running down of energy within this society. This entropic tendency towards decline is magnificently embodied in the opening lines:

        So all day long the noise of battle roll'd
        Among the mountains by the winter sea;
        Until King Arthur's table, man by man,
        Had fallen in Lyonnesse about their Lord,
        King Arthur: then, because his wound was deep,
        The bold Sir Bedivere uplifted him,
        Sir Bedivere, the last of all his knights,
        And bore him to a chapel nigh the field,
        A broken chancel with a broken cross,
        That stood on a dark strait of barren land.

The emphasis upon the broken relics of religion hints both at Tennyson's personal crisis of faith after the death of Hallam and at that more widespread loss of faith which undermined the certitude of the Victorians. The depth of the wound attests also to the wound of the poetic creator here, the possibility of the text itself undercut by the very doubts and grief which give it its unifying resonance. Linguistically the poet strives for control and distancing of the highly emotional material he is dealing with. The underlying drift of the poem is towards passive acceptance of suffering, and there is a curious and disturbing gap in the poem between the richness of the landscape evocations and the stiffly hieratic figures of the participants, who act as if drained of humanity. Ricks speaks of 'the disconcerting play of a sharply visualized setting against a central vacancy', and claims to detect a rupture between the deepest emotional reactions conjured up by the descriptions of the landscape and the stereotypes imaged in the protagonists. Certainly there does appear to be 'the wound of a fracture' in the text itself, in the words of Paul de Man, which both echoes and distorts the wound suffered by the king. The project of the poem is strangely undermined by this central vacancy: it tries to imagine loss, but can do so only by a severely repressed process of dissociation, by projecting emotional loss and inertia on to the landscape and endowing Sir Bedivere with a bluff common sense far removed from the poet's own feelings at this time. The ultimately unresolvable dialectic between loss and hope is beautifully caught in the final lines:

> ... Long stood Sir Bedivere
> Revolving many memories, till the hull
> Look'd one black dot against the verge of dawn,
> And on the mere the wailing died away.

The ambiguity leaves the way open for either optimistic or pessimistic interpretation, the poem inserting itself with an ambiguous power within the mind of the reader.


### 'Break, break, break ...' (1842)

This poem was written one spring morning in Lincolnshire, probably in 1834. In this lament over Hallam's death, the regularity and funereal rhythms of 'Break, break, break' frame the poem with a resonant sadness. The poem seems to be striving to verbalize a meaning which remains resolutely unsayable:

> And I would that my tongue could utter
> The thoughts that arise in me.

The light tripping rhythm here lays bare the impossibility of the poet's revealing his own deepest thoughts. The breaking of the waves encompasses the children on the shore, the sailor lad in the bay, and the stately ships moving towards 'their haven under the hill'. The speaker's anguish of loss reaches its climax in his sense of one who will never return, in a statement underlined by cleverly varying the three-beat rhythm into a four-stressed line:

> But O for the touch of a vanish'd hand,
> And the sound of a voice that is still!

The three figures perceived in the longer perspective are pursuing untroubled lives, and yet the 'O well' hints at some portent lying over their future also. The Victorian critic R. H. Hutton well defined the poem as one where Tennyson turns 'an ordinary sea-shore landscape into a means of finding a voice indescribably sweet for the dumb spirit of human loss'.

The 'plot' of the poem is difficult to unravel, despite the deceptive simplicity of diction and verse-form. There is here a sense of something hidden from both speaker and listener. We are invited to make out a state of mind from the seascape, but it is as though the meaning of the text is always just vanishing over the horizon like the ships it describes. Ricks suggests that the 'Ands' and 'Buts' signify a disjunction between a literal and figurative mode of utterance, a desire to make connections which in fact are never achieved. Sinfield counters with the observation that these connectives 'can be held, with equal consistency, either to demand symbolic reading or to expose that demand'. There is considerable play upon the act of utterance: the poet's tongue cannot 'utter', the children 'shout', the sailor 'sings', and the poet longs for the 'sound of a voice that is still'. Human loss is thought of as silence, and placed against the implacable regularity of nature, the almost mindless joy of the shouting and singing contrasted with the delicacy of 'the touch of a vanish'd hand' which serves to suggest the softness of the voice that is lost for ever. Voice implies full presence, but as so often in Tennyson, that presence is already lost in the prehistory of the text. The act of writing, inscribing marks upon the page, is a foredoomed attempt to bring back speech. Writing, by its very nature, implies distance, so that the heartbreak is already inscribed in the formation of words upon the page: language itself attempts always to fill (unsuccessfully) the gap left through desire.

It has been suggested that the last lines represent a kind of resolution of the tensions of the poem, but they seem rather to sustain the poem in its mood of agonized realization of the finality of loss. The speaker is distanced not only from the thoughtless joy of the playing children but also from the bleak anonymity of the sea itself. The point of the poem lies, therefore, in its realization of pointlessness.

# 6. 'Locksley Hall' (1842)

Tennyson composed this poem, written in 1837–8, in long, swinging eight-stressed trochaic lines, recalling how Hallam's father told him 'that the English people liked verse in trochaics'. The hero wishes to escape out of his present intolerable situation into a life of irresponsibility: 'Ah, for some retreat/ Deep in yonder shining Orient, where my life began to beat'. He never decides finally whether he is to join the evolving 'Mother-Age' or blow it up in a revolutionary act of vandalism. Yet the poem does bear witness to Tennyson's shared enthusiasm for many of the Victorian beliefs in progress and mechanical inventions:

Men, my brothers, men the workers, ever reaping something new:
That which they have done but earnest of the things that they shall do:

The speaker is one with the 'standards of the people' and embraces 'that one increasing purpose'. But this purpose seems not to embrace the Great House, which is inhabited by unpleasant gentry. The 'social lies' and 'sickly forms' of this class are contrasted with the energy of the captains of industry in a way which is familiar to readers of Victorian fiction of the period. Indeed, the poem envisions a future in which the activities of commerce are triumphant. This joyous note of mastery over nature is juxtaposed with a dissonant note of disturbance and violence: the hero longs to perish 'falling on the foeman's ground', and in his vision of the future he includes air battles, 'ghastly dew/ From the nations' airy navies grappling in the central blue'. In this imminent apocalypse the hero wishes to discover an ideal death where the 'ranks are roll'd in vapour, and the winds are laid with sound'. The poem thus contrives to suggest a balance between contrary forces: the disappointed lover first bemoans the faithlessness of his still loved Amy, then his love is countered by hatred of her. He merges these emotions dangerously as he comes to visualize her life with a brutalized husband. This synthesis then marks the beginning of a new opposition, as he turns to celebrate the achievements of the age. Towards the end, he appears to have gained self-confidence and a sense of purpose, but this remains undermined by the rhythms of the verse itself. Tennyson's undisclosed project may have been to exorcize his rejection by Rosa Baring of Harrington Hall, and this brings with it a claustrophobic sense of empathy between writer and hero, both in the matter of unrequited love and in the railing against a pretentious aristocracy, where references to the ambitions of the Tennyson d'Eyncourts of Bayons Manor may be detected. The poet claimed, 'The whole poem represents young life, its good side, its deficiencies, and its yearnings', but this bland assurance masks an evasiveness at the heart of the text, and a notable lack of coherence in the character of the imagined speaker. What, for instance, is the reader to make of such outbursts as this:

> Well – 'tis well that I should bluster! – Hadst thou less unworthy
> proved –
> Would to God – for I had loved thee more than ever wife was
> loved.
>
> Am I mad, that I should cherish that which bears but bitter fruit?
> I will pluck it from my bosom, tho' my heart be at the root.

This is the speaking voice of an egotist, but the long-drawn-out couplets tend to dissipate the force and vehemence of his utterance. The speaker tries to project himself as a man who, though wounded by his early experiences of life, is still full of energy. Recollection of his early years is interrupted by the tale of his love affair, and he returns again to this part of his life after a lengthy section devoted exclusively to wild invective.

The speaker in fact *retreats* into his dream of the future; it represents a comfort not available to him at this moment:

> When I dipt into the future far as human eye could see,
> Saw the Vision of the world, and all the wonder that would be.

There appears to be an inner conflict between the different voices of the speaker himself, and the almost symphonic attempt to arrange these voices is part of the strange appeal of 'Locksley Hall'. Born with a strong faith in the future, the speaker has been embittered by social injustice, and is now torn between a soul-destroying bitterness and a desire to join in with the Victorian 'march of mind'. His deep-seated problem (and that of his creator) is to regain a sense of visionary wonder, and it is that wonder which he apparently recovers when he exclaims, 'Ancient founts of inspiration well thro' all my fancy yet'. Disappointed by Amy's capitulation to 'the social wants that sin against the strength of youth', the speaker seeks to travel, but cannot evade the truth that the values which led Amy to marry are centrally Victorian. Trade itself may be romanticized, as when the speaker sees 'the heavens fill with commerce, argosies of magic sails'. In such lines poetry seems able to transmute the brutal force of the new mechanisms of commerce and utility, and allows the speaker to indulge a childish fantasy of universal peace:

> Till the war-drum throbb'd no longer, and the battle-flags were furled
> In the Parliament of man, the Federation of the world.

But danger lurks at home, with the Chartist threat to stability and order:

> Slowly comes a hungry people, as a lion creeping nigher,
> Glares at one that nods and winks behind a slowly-dying fire.

Such threats combined with his personal anguish lead the hero into palpably strong fantasies of escape, in which, as often in Tennyson, classical allusion creates a deep, if hidden, resonance:

> Or to burst all links of habit – there to wander far away,
> On from island unto island at the gateways of the day.

> Larger constellations burning, mellow moons and happy skies,
> Breadths of tropic shade and palms in cluster, knots of Paradise.

> Never comes the trader, never floats an European flag,
> Slides the bird o'er lustrous woodland, swings the trailer from the crag;

> Droops the heavy-blossom'd bower, hangs the heavy-fruited tree –
> Summer isles of Eden lying in dark-purple spheres of sea.

But the text cannot easily sacrifice the evolutionary notion of European supremacy, counting the 'gray barbarian lower than the Christian child', and the hero is made to wish to live in full harmony with the doctrine of progress, in an image curiously distorted from the new age of railway travel: 'Let the great world spin for ever down the ringing grooves of change'. Such vaunting assertiveness collapses in upon itself with the final storm, and the prayer that it should fall upon Locksley Hall itself; here, we feel, is one genuine voice of the protagonist seeking freedom in a conclusion which is simultaneously a fantasy of vengeance and release.

Sinfield's interpretation of the poem as revealing, beneath the social critique, Tennyson's complicity in the vast historical process of colonial subjugation and exploitation is worth pondering by every reader. Another reading may be offered, however, which addresses the problematic of the speaking voice. The overwhelming effect of reading 'Locksley Hall' is of contact with a disconnected sensibility, of not one but many voices producing a 'layered' effect in the text. In that sense the poem is curiously modern, since the reader can scarcely detect any unifying subject behind an 'I' which progressively unravels itself as the poem proceeds. The gaps in the subjectivity of the speaker are dizzyingly multiple: there is the voice which speaks idyllically of youth, the voice which vituperates the cousin, 'shallow-hearted', and rails against 'the gold that gilds the straitened forehead of the fool', the voice which hails social progress, 'men, the workers, ever reaping something new', the voice which longs for indolent ease, and the voice demanding the obliteration of Locksley Hall. These disjunctive voices serve to hint at a vertiginous loss of any unifying sensibility able to endow its experience with meaning. Every mood is negated, so that meanings multiply and cancel each other out in a re-enactment of the splitting of the subject itself. The unified self beloved of Victorian art – as of economic and social theory – here crashes noisily to the ground. The reader is aware of an uncomfortable lack or absence at the heart of the poem, a lack which arises out of the liberal-humanist contradictions of the author's own situation. If the subject is constructed through the gap between the 'I' who is the speaker and the 'I' who is spoken of, then the poem suggests that the gap can never successfully be negotiated. The 'subject', as analysed by Catherine Belsey, sounds remarkably close to the hero of 'Locksley Hall':

Unfixed, unratified, the human being is not a unity, not autonomous, but a process, perpetually in construction, perpetually contradictory, perpetually open to change.[10]

'Locksley Hall', that is to say, acts out some of the disturbing implications of the modernist decentred subject, and that enactment focuses upon the most crucial under-text of Victorian literature, human sexuality. 'Locksley Hall' dramatizes a range of feelings and responses which centre hysterically around the hero's sexuality. The appeal to male comradeship at the opening:

Comrades, leave me here a little, while as yet 'tis early morn:
Leave me here, and when you want me, sound upon the bugle-horn.

consorts revealingly with a pervasive jealousy towards, and fear of, women. Amy is at once the centre of the obsessive male glance, deliberately reversed in the exhibitionistic 'her eyes on all my motions with a mute observance hung', and simultaneously an object of jealousy and contempt who leads the hero into a willed fantasy of erotic death:

Better thou and I were lying, hidden from the heart's disgrace,
Roll'd in one another's arms, and silent in a last embrace.

We are scarcely surprised to hear Amy instructed a little later:

> Woman is the lesser man, and all thy passions, match'd with mine,
> Are as moonlight unto sunlight, and as water unto wine –

The deep-rooted fascination with, and fear of, sexuality, especially female, is made explicit in the atavistic section which envisages a return to 'savagery' through constructing an Other which directly opposes the social identity of the Victorian male, who is to be mated, 'with a squalid savage'. Such dangerous sexuality may be sublimated through the heroic engagement with the dogma of progress:

> Better fifty years of Europe than a cycle of Cathay

and through the revealing return to a pre-sexual nirvana in the invocation to the 'Mother-Age'.

The splintered personae of modern literature – Strindberg's 'split and vacillating' characters – are already present here and in *Maud*, and in both texts the author circles warily around a sexual imbroglio. 'Locksley Hall' indeed bespeaks an explicit concern, albeit confused and contradictory, with problems of sexual feeling. In this regard, both 'Locksley Hall' and *Maud* constitute useful documentation of Michel Foucault's argument that sexuality, 'far from undergoing a process of restriction' in the nineteenth century, 'on the contrary has been subjected to a mechanism of increasing incitement'.[11] Foucault believes that, in contradistinction to the accepted view of Victorian morality, there occurred a 'multiplication of discourses concerning sex in the field of exercise of power itself', 'a determination on the part of the agencies of power to hear it spoken about, and to cause *it* to speak through explicit articulation and endlessly accumulated detail'. There existed within an epoch 'dominated by (highly prolix) directives enjoining modesty and discretion', 'a plurisecular injunction to talk about sex'. In Foucault's reading, there is a sexuality of 'spaces' – the school, the prison, the home – and it is precisely such topographical sexuality which 'Locksley Hall' releases and feeds upon in its contrastively pure sea-coast where the speaker 'wander'd, nourishing a youth sublime' and the snobbish Hall, with its imagined sacrificial sexual victim, 'mated with a clown'.

The poet's nervousness in his concern with a hidden yet explicit sexuality engenders the extreme oscillations of voice within this poem and *Maud*. The speaker of 'Locksley Hall', benefiting from the Grundyish disposition of his supposed audience, is compelled to bypass his sexual fantasies in favour of bellicose pre-natal language and metaphor. The language of sexuality, when not permitted explicit statement, is enriched through indirection, symbol and figuration. As George

Steiner observes, 'Sexual relations are, or should be, one of the citadels of privacy, the night-place where we must be allowed to gather the splintered, harried elements of our consciousness.'[12] It is precisely this 'splintered, harried' self which 'Locksley Hall' so strangely imagines and projects in its disintegrating cacophony of voices.

# 7. Selected Lyrics from *The Princess* (1847)

### 1. 'As thro' the land'

This song employs the image of the child which is to reverberate through a number of the lyrics in *The Princess*. Husband and wife fall out as they walk through the wheat fields, but 'kiss again with tears' when they come upon the grave of their dead child. This child becomes, within the lyric, a force for unity and reconciliation. The idea of the child also works as a natural symbol which incites the kisses here and awakens Ida's sexuality in the main poem itself. The lyric suggests that a unity which follows disunity is all the stronger: 'And blessings on the falling out/ That all the more endears'.

### 2. 'Sweet and low'

Another subtle evocation of the binding force of the child with a context of sexual love. The father is drawn back from the 'dying moon' to his life at the hearth, significantly not so much by the wife's pleas in the first stanza as by the 'babe in the nest' of the second stanza. Rhythmically, the poem subtly suggests the ebb and flow of the sea, and the rocking of the cradle.

### 3. 'The splendour falls'

One of the poet's most remarkable exercises in onomatopoeia. The heroic echoes of the bugle call fade gradually away, 'answer, echoes, dying, dying, dying', whilst the personal 'echoes' of human lives 'grow for ever and for ever' through time. Fame does not combat time, the lyric suggests, thus denying the drift of Princess Ida's argument, but human love and continuity are immortal.

### 4. 'Tears, idle tears'

This grave and elegiac poem was composed, Tennyson recalled, at Tintern Abbey. He held that it expressed 'the yearning that young people occasionally experience for that which seems to have passed away for ever'. In another comment, the poet remarked, 'It is the sense of the abiding in the transient.' The reader may not immediately notice here the absence of any rhyme, but this is significant since the poem is predicated upon the fact of absence in various modes. Despite the blank-verse form the reader has somehow a general impression of rhyme from a reading of the lyric. There is a disjunction in the text concerning what exactly it is that is lost to the speaker – whether it is the 'public' arena of history or the private history of an individual existence. Yet the poem successfully mobilizes both senses of loss and pastness.

In a famous discussion of the poem, Cleanth Brooks[13] argues that the poem is one of a subtlety and ambiguity unusual with Tennyson. The 'idleness' of the tears prompts Brooks to argue that the poem begins in paradox, since these tears in fact 'rise in the heart' from some divine despair. The tears rise as the speaker gazes upon the 'happy Autumn-fields' and thinks back to the days that are no more, the autumnal note suggesting, like Keats's ode, something which is irrevocably over and finished. In the second stanza, Brooks observes, it is no surprise to learn that the days that are no more are 'sad', but there is a sense of shock in hearing them described as 'fresh', and that adjective is then applied to the light on the sails of the boat. Whilst the 'underworld' seems here appropriately to suggest the antipodes whence the boat is travelling, the word of course also carries the freight of its classical suggestion about the abode of the dead, and this deathly overtone modifies and distorts the effect of 'fresh' with renewed power and ambiguity. The light on the sail of the boat suggests both joy and then sadness as the ship 'sails with all we love below the verge'. In the third stanza the dawn scene is also riven with ambiguity, since it is a dawn perceived through the eyes of a dying man. As Brooks remarks, 'the images from the past rise up with a strange clarity and sharpness that shock the speaker'. There is an intensity about the text which is at odds with its elegiac theme, and this intensity climaxes in the final stanza, beginning 'Dear as remember'd kisses after death'. In its passionate cry, 'O Death in Life, the days that are no more', Brooks detects a richness and complexity of verbal organization more characteristic of modernist poetry in its riddling ambiguity. In a response to Brooks's reading, Leo Spitzer[14] concentrates upon the 'divine despair', and sees this as the informing principle of the poem, which then allows a sense of deity into the text. The poem is built upon a duality, in this reading, inherent in the epithets selected by the poet 'in his impotent revolt against reawakened sensations'. This dualism is registered in the phrases 'fresh but sad', 'sad but strange', 'dear, sweet, deep, but wild'. The contradictions raised here, Spitzer claims, 'leave us indeed in deep despair as to the irrevocably antithetic nature of the

71

Janus-like God' who rules the universe. Through such means, both critics agree, a triumphant piece of art is made out of human despair.

### 5. 'Now sleeps the crimson petal'

This beautiful and erotic song, based upon Persian models, is sung to herself by Ida when she is reconsidering the Prince's proposal. It is a highly structured poem, and its meaning absolutely depends upon a cluster of differences and correspondences. The repeated 'Now' of the first line suggests both simultaneity and alternatives, and that sense of uncertainty is preserved in the relationship between 'Now' and the echoic 'Nor'. The first three lines stress an absence of movement in an atmosphere which is pervasively somnolent and passive. As Sinfield points out, in line four the woman participates in both the stillness of the first three lines and in the awakening movement of the firefly. The 'glimmering' of the white peacock probably echoes a similar moment in Shelley's 'The Triumph of Life'. In both texts polarities of light and dark are somehow matched up with waking and sleeping states: light covers light, trance covers slumber, so as to create optical confusions which enact the very process of reading the poem itself, where meanings are veiled from the reader. The effects are masked, tantalizingly erotic within an ambivalent word-pattern. The image of the peacock leads on to the more dynamic image of the meteor:

> Now slides the silent meteor on, and leaves
> A shining furrow, as thy thoughts in me.

As Sinfield points out, 'the male speaker, without moving, has absorbed' his beloved. But the metaphor also speaks of the condition of writing itself, of the way the inscription of the pen leaves a 'silent furrow' upon the page, in a crucial linguistic re-enactment of sexual love. The poem ends with a successful, restorative cancelling of difference and separation:

> Now folds the lily all her sweetness up,
> And slips into the bosom of the lake:
> So fold thyself, my dearest, thou, and slip
> Into my bosom and be lost in me.

### 6. 'Come down, O maid'

Tennyson composed this poem of the mountain heights whilst travelling in Switzerland in 1846. As Ricks remarks, it is a poem of 'courteous seduction':

> What pleasure lives in height (the shepherd sang)
> In height and cold, the splendour of the hills?

Height and cold are set antithetically against the warmth and nurturing shelter of the lowlands, since 'Love is of the valley'. To the lover the heights are cold and sterile, but Tennyson qualifies this view with his romantic portrayal of dark Alpine forests, the cry of the eagles, and the 'blasted Pine'. None the less, the poem does finally endorse, in its magically evocative ending, the inviting sensuousness of natural love:

> Sweeter thy voice, but every sound is sweet;
> Myriads of rivulets hurrying thro' the lawn,
> The moan of doves in immemorial elms,
> And murmuring of innumerable bees.

# *In Memoriam A.H.H.* (1850)

## Form and Structure

Tennyson's most famous work was essentially a compilation, as was clearly indicated by the original title, 'Fragments of an Elegy'. This title is apposite, since on one level the poem deals with a fragmented personality trying to pick up the pieces after a shattering loss. *In Memoriam* is best read, not at a sitting, but as a series of poems composed at various times after the news of Hallam's death in 1833 right up to the time of the work's completion in 1849. Some of the lyrics were composed as free-standing pieces, whilst others were arranged sequentially by the poet. Ultimately, however, Tennyson arranged the material in a homogeneous manner, irrespective of date of composition, in order to present the reader with a portrayal of crisis, loss and renewal of faith. As a whole the poem moves slowly but inexorably towards a mood of greater assurance, reflecting perhaps Tennyson's suggested sub-title, 'The Way of the Soul'. By working his way from the early riveting reflections upon death and loss to the marriage poem, the work gains a semblance of unity it might not otherwise possess.

Dates of composition are not known with any certainty, but amongst the earliest sections completed were 9, 28, 30 and 31; at the other end of the scale, 39 was not incorporated into the text until 1869. The Epilogue, concerning Tennyson's sister Cecilia's marriage to Edmund Lushington, was composed in 1842, and the framing Prologue in 1849. Commentators have sought to impose unity upon the diversity of the text in various ways. It has been suggested, for instance, that the Christmas poems, 28–30, 78, 104–6, mark crucial phases of the poet's development, or alternatively that the sections marking the anniversaries of Hallam's death, 72 and 99, are the turning points in the argument. It is perhaps more useful to the reader in keeping her bearings to adhere to the poet's own suggested grouping into nine parts, as follows:

### i Sections 1–8

This is a grief-stricken opening sequence which already adumbrates the evolutionary scheme of the whole, since it suggests that the poet is as yet unable to rise above his grief towards a renewed sense of life. The poet envies the graveyard yew tree, but gains some comfort from the 'sad mechanic exercise' of writing, and he proceeds to wrap himself in words like 'coarsest clothes against the cold'. This section reaches its apogee in the desolate approach to the Hallams' London house in Wimpole Street.

## ii Sections 9–20

The second section speaks more calmly of the death of Hallam, and reveals a less intensely neurotic sensibility. Tennyson imaginatively follows the course of the ship carrying Hallam's body back to the Severn. Although a greater calm does prevail, there are still rapid alternations of feeling between this calm and a wild despair.

## iii Sections 21–27

The poem moves into a more pastoral mode at this point. Tennyson recalls walks and intellectual converse with his friend at Somersby, through 'four sweet years' before death intervened. He reflects that it is 'better to have loved and lost' than never to have experienced this relationship.

## iv Sections 28–49

A time of recovery begins tentatively with the Christmas bells. Despite the family's grief, the customs of Christmas Eve are carefully observed at Somersby, and Christmas Day becomes associated with a slight rebirth of hope. The story of Lazarus is parabolically alluded to, and Tennyson reflects upon our ignorance of the life after death. Without a sense of immortality, the poet now begins to feel, life itself would be worthless. Although the following spring brings with it little renewal of joy, the poet does now feel that the dead live in a higher realm, and that he may, one day, be reunited with his beloved friend. Individuality, it seems, will be retained after death, until all are submerged within the 'general soul'.

## v Sections 50–58

Doubt and uncertainty crowd in again upon the poet. His language is inadequate to the emotion he feels, but he trusts that somehow good will finally triumph. Abandoning the brave philosophical stance, he confesses he is no better than 'An infant crying for the light'. Nature, read according to the proto-evolutionary doctrine of such works as Lyell's

*Principles of Geology*, undermines the poet's faith: she seems blatantly indifferent to the valued individual and even to entire species. Man, Tennyson reflects bleakly, may end 'blown about the desert dust,/ Or sealed within the iron hills'. The poet is convinced that his grief will always remain, tolling in his mind like a 'set slow bell', but his poetic inspiration leads him towards patience and self-command.

## vi Sections 59–71

In this sequence the poet reflects that some kind of communication may be possible with the dead Hallam. He feels that his friend is watching over him, and as the moonlight falls upon the poet's bed he thinks of an almost mystical light illuminating Hallam's memorial in the church at Clevedon. Hallam now appears to him in a series of dreams, including one in which he advises the poet that his grief is not unmanly, and another in which Tennyson recollects their journey to the Pyrenees together.

## vii Sections 72–98

Reflections upon the greatness of Hallam start up in the poet's mind on the cold anniversary of his death in Vienna. The second Christmas passes calmly, but with a deep sense of regret and loss still numbing the poet's mind. Tennyson explains to his favourite brother Charles why it is that the poet's love for Hallam is different from his brotherly feelings, and goes on to speculate as to how Hallam's career would have developed had the latter lived. He extends a friendly hand to Edmund Lushington, who is to become his brother-in-law. After a calming interlude at Barmouth on the Welsh coast, Tennyson feels able to return to Cambridge, where he vividly recalls Hallam's abilities in debate and intellectual argument. He re-creates more intimately happy scenes at Somersby. Reading a letter late at night on the rectory lawn, the poet has a sudden poignant vision of his friend. The section ends with a refusal to visit the city of Vienna.

## viii Sections 99–103

This section records the departure of the Tennysons from Somersby in the spring of 1837. Landscapes made doubly dear to the poet through their association with Hallam merge into 'one pure image of regret' as Tennyson leaves his native Lincolnshire. Christmas feels strange in the new house at Epping, but the New Year bells are implored to ring in a new life for the poet, and for mankind at large.

### ix Sections 104–131

In the final sequence, Tennyson seeks to show how death is swallowed up in the victory of faith. Reflecting again upon what Hallam might have become leads the poet to recognize that intellect is not sufficient to bring man wisdom. With the coming of another spring his regret blossoms into a longing for some more potent bond 'which is to be' with Hallam. The maturing of the individual, he realizes, is part and parcel of a wider evolutionary process. He is now able to visit Wimpole Street in a calmer frame of mind. The planet, visualized as 'sad Hesper', the evening star, prepared to die with the buried sun, has become Phosphor, the morning star. The evidence of the rocks does not now challenge the poet's conviction that God is love, and that all is well with the universe. Despite fluctuating 'eddies in the flood/ Of onward time', the human race will continue its upward progress, with all 'toil coöperant to an end'. Hallam is a noble type, born ahead of his time, and now at one with the deity. *In Memoriam* ends with a lengthy Epilogue, celebrating the marriage of Edmund Lushington and Cecilia Tennyson.

### The Personal Element

Tennyson was to claim some years after the composition and publication of *In Memoriam* that the poem was 'rather the cry of the whole human race than mine'. But he also added, 'It's too hopeful, this poem, more than I am myself.' *In Memoriam* is surely only universal in the sense that it confronts the universal fact of, and response to, the experience of bereavement. If the poem does possess any claims to universality, it also possesses extreme privacy and intimacy of utterance; its confused project, that is to say, is to be both an elegiac and a philosophical poem. The question which often confronts the reader of so long a work is whether the verse form is as suitable to the attempts at philosophical statement as it is to personal elegy. As Ricks has said, the work is 'anonymous but confessional, private but naked'.

Tennyson begins from a position of having to reject well-meaning comforters:

> One writes, that 'Other friends remain,'
> That 'Loss is common to the race' –

> And common is the commonplace.
> And vacant chaff well meant for grain.
>
> (6)

The opening sections, dominated by the old churchyard yew and the dark house in London, lead Tennyson to imagine the finality of 'A hand that can be clasp'd no more'. The statement 'He is not here', of the dark house poem, with its reverberant echo of the Resurrection, both undermines and re-imagines the confines of the poet's grief. The unconscious, and especially the dream-world, exerts a dominant hold upon the poet in this dreadful situation. The dream may take many forms. It can be deceptive, such as that of the widower:

> . . . when he sees
> A late-lost form that sleep reveals,
> And moves his doubtful arms, and feels
> Her place is empty,
>
> (13)

or it may take the form of nightmare:

> But what is this? I turn about
> I find a trouble in thine eye,
> Which makes me sad I know not why,
> Nor can my dream resolve the doubt:
>
> (68)

or the later, more calming and quasi-Arthurian vision of Hallam with the maidens, in section 103.

In conscious waking life Tennyson inevitably associates his dead friend with specific times and places: the bleak confrontation with the London house, the visit to Cambridge with its 'reverend walls' (87), and the aversion to Vienna, full of a 'treble darkness' (98), are all carefully woven into the texture of the memories the poem conjures up from time to time. But most crucially the poem centres upon Somersby as the 'beloved place' where Hallam was to be indissolubly linked to the Tennyson clan:

> Witch-elms that counterchange the floor
> Of this flat lawn with dusk and bright;
> And thou, with all thy breadth and height
> Of foliage, towering sycamore;

> How often, hither wandering down,
>     My Arthur found your shadows fair,
>     And shook to all the liberal air
> The dust and din and steam of town:

(89)

It is this deep familial association which will create the sadness of the final departure from Lincolnshire for the poet; here there is 'no place that does not breathe/ Some gracious memory of my friend':

> No gray old grange, or lonely fold,
>     Or low morass and whispering reed,
>     Or simple stile from mead to mead,
> Or sheepwalk up the windy wold;

(100)

The first Christmas after Hallam's death Tennyson 'slept and woke with pain' and almost 'wish'd no more to wake' (28), but with the family at Somersby he had continued mechanically to weave 'the holly round the Christmas hearth' (30). Following the removal from Somersby he hears only bells he no longer recognizes:

> Like strangers' voices here they sound,
>     In lands where not a memory strays,
>     Nor landmark breathes of other days,
> But all is new unhallow'd ground.

(104)

Beside such natural ruminations upon the for ever vanished past stand fantasies and projections about the different future that might have been had Hallam lived. At first, Tennyson is almost unable to believe the fact of death:

> If one should bring me this report,
>     That thou hadst touch'd the land today,
>     And I went down unto the quay,
> And found thee lying in the port;

(14)

As time moves on Tennyson gains strength by comparing his feelings at the death of his friend with what Hallam's would have been if the situation had been reversed:

> Then fancy shapes, as fancy can,
>     The grief my loss in him had wrought,

> A grief as deep as life or thought,
> But stay'd in peace with God and man.

(80)

Such fantasies develop so that the poet imagines Hallam married to his sister Emily, and with children towards whom the poet would be uncle:

> I seem to meet their least desire
> To clap their cheeks, to call them mine.
> I see their unborn faces shine
> Beside the never-lighted fire.

(84)

Yet the poet's relationship with Hallam does not depend solely upon such hapless imaginings. The poem claims to be the vehicle for a continuing 'commerce with the dead' (85), but the nobility of the dead man shows up dark faults in the poet of which he is ashamed:

> Do we indeed desire the dead
> Should still be near us at our side?
> Is there no baseness we would hide?
> No inner vileness that we dread?

(51)

Notwithstanding such moments of self-knowledge, the poem seeks always the closest relation with the dead, and that seeking culminates in the visionary ecstasy of section 95. In such moods Tennyson has progressed beyond the loneliness he has earlier given voice to in the sense of a chilling 'spectral doubt' (41).

Now, towards the end of the poem, the voice sounds more hopeful, trusting that those whom 'we call the dead' live in constant communion with the living. The claims of 124, about the feeling heart which is never extinguished by grief, lead inexorably to the hymn-like climax:

> Love is and was my Lord and King,
> And in his presence I attend
> To hear the tidings of my friend,
> Which every hour his couriers bring.

(126)

Yet there is, for the reader finely attuned to the verse, a willed impersonality here which consorts ill with the deepest and most personal parts of what is, at bottom, a deeply personal utterance in poetic form.

**The Poetic Pattern**

In section 96, which was added later to the text of 1850, the poet explains how the visionary presence of Hallam, sought so intensely in the previous section, had come to him, and how it was to be read as the climactic moment of the entire work, exemplifying the triumph of faith over doubt:

> He faced the spectres of the mind
> And laid them: thus he came at length
>
> To find a stronger faith his own;
>   And Power was with him in the night,
>   Which makes the darkness and the light,
> And dwells not in the light alone,
>
> (96)

The poem, that is to say, depends for its success upon a reconciliation of light and dark elements in human life; in general terms, the poem moves towards the light and away from the opening darkness. The anguish of the opening sequence must contain the seeds of hope, but that hope is often lost sight of in the vacillations of mood which *In Memoriam* records so plangently. The violent fluctuations of mood, indeed, serve to expose the lack of a sense of an organizing principle in life itself. The new sense of hope is particularly marked in the mood of renewal announced in the pivotal section 57, where the 'song of woe' is gradually subdued.

The relaxation here still contains and refers to the vehemence of an earlier despair and anguish, but there is a new note of acceptance in language which now seeks to express a mastery of the fact of death. Section 57 is indeed central as a turning point, the moment where the suffering of the first half is transforming itself into something more relaxed and humane. That reversal also works more pervasively in the text; the images of nature as a pre-Darwinian battleground which dominate the first half are transmuted into images of harmony, as the poet grapples to show that human love does indeed have a value and permanence transcending death.

The poem begins by rejecting what it will later affirm – the rebirth of the self. There is at this stage a virtual absence of feeling which is further developed in the yew-tree lyric. Here the Romantic doctrine of unity with nature is rewritten with nightmarish effect:

> And gazing on thee, sullen tree,
>   Sick for thy stubborn hardihood,
>   I seem to fail from out my blood
> And grow incorporate into thee.
>
> (2)

The yew is to return, in one of the reiterative images of the poem, in section 39, where the poet now acknowledges the part played by the tree in the natural cycle:

> Dark yew, that graspest at the stones
>
> And dippest toward the dreamless head,
>   To thee too comes the golden hour
>   When flower is feeling after flower;
>
> (39)

Generally, however, in the first movement of the poem nature's potency deceives, since man is now banished from its restorative cycles. The beautiful Lincolnshire landscape of section 11 lulls the reader into a false sense of security:

> Calm and still light on yon great plain
>   That sweeps with all its autumn bowers,
>   And crowded farms and lessening towers,
> To mingle with the bounding main:

Perception of the outer scene, however, is not matched by inner feeling, and the verse proceeds to undermine and displace this calming effect, with its final emphasis upon that 'calm despair' (11).

Equally, the meditation on the Severn in section 19 works through an ironic reversal of the traditional pastoral mode:

> The Danube to the Severn gave
>   The darken'd heart that beat no more;
>   They laid him by the pleasant shore,
> And in the hearing of the wave.
>
> (19)

The water which hushes the Wye parallels the deep grief of the narrator, and as the tide recedes it releases only grief and sorrow. In section 23, 'Now, sometimes in my sorrow shut', we are presented with a past in which the poet and Hallam were blood-brothers, completely attuned to natural life. This was a time when 'all the secret of the Spring/ Moved in the chambers of the blood'. This past plenitude and togetherness is implicitly contrasted with the desolate present, but then the following section rewrites this by questioning our idealization of the past: 'was the day of my delight/ As pure and perfect as I say?' The entire first movement of the poem implies that the pain which is faced may be a necessary catharsis, and this is of course acknowledged in the famous couplet, ''Tis better to have loved and lost/ Than never to have loved at all' (27). Love may be fully experienced only through loss and absence, and this recognition leads to a gradual lightening of the gloom:

> My own dim life should teach me this,
>   That life shall live for evermore,
>   Else earth is darkness at the core,
> And dust and ashes all that is;
>
> (34)

It has been interestingly suggested that the affirmative elements of the poem are presented indirectly, through image and metaphor, and that its negatives are stated baldly and directly. Whilst this is sometimes the case, it does not apply to the poetic pattern as a whole. If death brings extinction of the self, then any consideration of the existence of God becomes an irrelevance. The greatest accusation to be brought against death is that it 'broke our fair companionship' (22), and it is the breakdown of the familial and communal which is at the heart of *In Memoriam*, a breakdown which leads the poet, in section 40, to try to assimilate the death of Hallam into a dramatic framework. The dead man is now compared with a bride on her wedding day, and his death to her leaving for a new life. But the analogy is forced and artificial, and soon disintegrates: 'Ay me, the difference I discern!/ How often shall her old fireside/ Be cheer'd with tidings of the bride'. However, the mood lightens in sections 41–9, which take the form of a sequence of meditations upon happier possibilities. For example: death may simply be a form of sleep; the dead may recall their friends; or the human personality may survive after death. In section 46 Tennyson indulges in the rather complex notion that death is really a window upon the past, so that the love he feels for Hallam is in a sense eternal: 'O Love, thy province were not large,/ A bounded field, nor stretching far;/ Look also, Love, a brooding star,/ A rosy warmth from marge to marge'. But all this is speculation, and it collapses abruptly into the overwhelmingly bleak stasis of section 50:

> Be near me when my light is low,
>   When the blood creeps, and the nerves prick

> And tingle; and the heart is sick,
> And all the wheels of Being slow.
>
> (50)

The heavy, clogged syllabic movement mimetically supports and endorses the argument that no change can matter now, and the reflections upon change lead directly into the evolutionary sections, 54–56. The first of these tries to affirm, but its affirmation is virtually lost in the horror of what it formally seeks to deny:

> That not a worm is cloven in vain;
> That not a moth with vain desire
> Is shrivell'd in a fruitless fire,
> Or but subserves another's gain.
>
> (54)

The poet is left 'An infant crying for the light:/ And with no language but a cry'. In section 55 the poet contemplates the pervasive ironies of evolution, and of a nature 'So careful of the type' yet 'careless of the single life'. Unable to divine the 'secret meaning' of such prodigal waste in nature the verse almost collapses, rallying only weakly:

> I stretch lame hands of faith, and grope,
> And gather dust and chaff, and call
> To what I feel is Lord of all,
> And faintly trust the larger hope.
>
> (55)

But even this faint trust is shattered in section 56, in which the poem most potently confronts the likelihood of a futile universe: behind the 'veil' lies an almost Beckett-like sense of futility and pointlessness, and yet at this nadir of the poem's fortunes, the word 'peace' ushers in a new and more bearable mood:

> Peace; come away: the song of woe
> Is after all an earthly song:
> Peace; come away: we do him wrong
> To sing so wildly: let us go.
>
> (57)

It is as if the second half of the poem were to be devoted to the project of a reconstruction of the self, a reconstruction which is tentative and always threatened with instability, but which parallels the act of composition of the text. Indeed, section 58 expresses the poet's concern lest

the pessimism of the poem thus far may affect his contemporaries too
deeply:

> The high Muse answer'd: 'Wherefore grieve
>   Thy brethren with a fruitless tear?
>   Abide a little longer here,
> And thou shalt take a nobler leave.'

In the succeeding sections the poet expresses a love approaching the
sexual for the dead Hallam, and proceeds to imagine his dead friend in a
series of different situations. This intimate sequence culminates in the
haunting evocation, in section 67, of Hallam's memorial tablet in the
church at Clevedon:

> When on my bed the moonlight falls,
>   I know that in thy place of rest
>   By that broad water of the west,
> There comes a glory on the walls:
>
> Thy marble bright in dark appears,
>   As slowly steals a silver flame
>   Along the letters of thy name,
> And o'er the number of thy years.
>
> The mystic glory swims away;
>   From off my bed the moonlight dies;
>   And closing eaves of wearied eyes
> I sleep till dusk is dipt in gray:
>
> And then I know the mist is drawn
>   A lucid veil from coast to coast,
>   And in the dark church like a ghost
> Thy tablet glimmers to the dawn.

(67)

The anniversary of Hallam's death, marked in section 72, by contrast
sinks back into the characteristic earlier mood of gloom and despondency
in its vision of a frozen and static nature, but section 80 restores the
balance by visualizing how Hallam himself would have turned the burden
of death 'into gain'. In section 83, 'Dip down upon the northern shore',
and especially in the fine Barmouth lyric (86), the poem seems to be once
more caught up within the larger rhythm of nature, and a note of renewal
is movingly sounded in the regenerative effects of the 'ambrosial air'.

Succeeding sections to some extent slip back from this hardly achieved peace, and once again the poem is haunted by a poignant sense of the physical absence of the beloved. In fact, however, the yearning which is expressed here for full presence is a preparation for the culmination of the entire poetic and biographical project, the vision of Arthur Hallam vouchsafed to the poet upon the Somersby lawn (95; to be examined below). Removal from Somersby (100–105) rather brutally breaks most of the strongest links with Hallam's memory and brings in its train a series of images of death, loss and transition. There are a number of suggested solutions to this state: at the Christmas party the family will 'drink to him, whate'er he be' – the festivity brusquely undermined by the almost horrible afterthought; or, alternatively, the poet determines not to cut himself off any longer from his fellows, but this larger sense of participation in the commonwealth slips hectically into the political diatribe of section 109, with its anger at the 'blind hysterics of the Celt'. *In Memoriam* is in danger of drifting out of control at this point, but regains a more equable and sensitive tone in the images of Hesper and Phosphor around which section 121 is organized. Here the poet seems to advocate a coalescence of past and present within a harmonious flow of time. Prior to this, Tennyson has deliberately echoed the deep gloom of the dark house section (7) with the more vibrant 'Doors, where my heart was used to beat'. In the sections in which the poem moves towards its peroration, Tennyson often indulges in dangerous generalization, as when he counsels men to 'Move upward, working out the beast,/ And let the ape and tiger die' (118). Yet underlying this somewhat vacuous version of the doctrine of progress, there is towards the close a more human and genuinely felt movement towards life and light. The Epilogue, cast in a different style, and seemingly resonant with a different voice, is controlled and certain in its effects, but it discovers that certainty in a characteristically public form of utterance far removed from the poem's most potent effects and meanings. The child to be born to Cecilia and Edmund Lushington is connected here with Arthur Hallam himself, and a teleological design is uncovered in the development of mankind, subject to 'one law' and moving inexorably towards the 'far-off divine event'.

Like the closing rhetoric of 'Ulysses', there is perhaps an element here of hypnotic self-persuasion which can never cancel out, for the perceptive reader of *In Memoriam*, that troubled and precarious sense of self which motivates the most inward parts of the poem. The poet has 'come through', and produced the text, but with a final declaration of assurance which undermines and unravels all surety.

**Section 95**

This crucial and centripetal section is subtly organized into four groups
of four stanzas, linked by such images as the recurrent 'white kine'. The
central stanzas are divided between the act of reading Hallam's letters
and the climactic vision of the dead man. Tennyson begins by providing
a calm and homely setting for his mystical experience; familial reality is
stressed, and the family 'we' is reassuring in its sense of commonality of
purpose and unity of life and memory. The whole family join in the
singing of the 'old songs', in an act which recapitulates and modulates
the episodes in sections 30 and 89 – moments of solace in the poet's
stuttering progress away from his grief. The opening landscape is peaceful:

>              . . . o'er the sky
> The silvery haze of summer drawn;
>
> And calm that let the tapers burn
>     Unwavering: not a cricket chirr'd:
>     The brook alone far-off was heard,
> And on the board the fluttering urn:

In section 93 Tennyson had muttered of Hallam, 'I shall not see thee',
but in 94 he reflects that the spirits of the dead may be contacted when
'thou too canst say,/ My spirit is at peace with all'. The occasion has,
therefore, been carefully prepared, and the lengthened vowels and voiced
consonants of the first two stanzas of section 95 serve to create a quality
of lightness and lack of movement which is further stressed by the verbs.
The following stanzas depict a more vivid movement, a sense of something impending:

> And bats went round in fragrant skies,
>     And wheel'd or lit the filmy shapes
>     That haunt the dusk, with ermine capes
> And woolly breasts and beaded eyes;
>
> While now we sang old songs that peal'd
>     From knoll to knoll, where, couch'd at ease,
>     The white kine glimmer'd, and the trees
> Laid their dark arms about the field.

The rhythms slowly grow more agitated, and the trees' 'dark arms'
recall to the reader's mind the earlier emphasis upon hands, hands which
act as emblems of the loss of the beloved, as in 'Reach out dead hands to
comfort me' (80). In stanza 5 Tennyson begins to isolate himself from

the familiar context; his brothers and sisters 'Withdrew themselves from me and night', the lights go out in the rectory, 'and I was all alone'. Tennyson turns to the letters of the dead man, 'those fall'n leaves which kept their green,/ The noble letters of the dead', cunningly echoing his earlier reflection upon Hallam, 'Thy leaf has perished in the green'. What is perused in these epistles makes a powerful impression: the act of reading, of interpreting the marks on the page, enunciates 'love's dumb cry defying change'. The letters themselves seem to be urging firmness of purpose to the vacillating poet:

> The faith, the vigour, bold to dwell
>   On doubts that drive the coward back,
>   And keen thro' wordy snares to track
> Suggestion to her inmost cell.

In this sense the act of reading the letters recapitulates the larger movement of the poem, moving from anxiety and stress towards emotional maturity and deliverance. But the basic impulse of the poem, the urgent desire for contact, is overwhelmingly felt:

> So word by word, and line by line,
>   The dead man touch'd me from the past,
>   And all at once it seem'd at last
> The living soul was flash'd on mine,

Tennyson's desire is here fulfilled in a momentary transcendent mystical experience in which the self is caught up within a circle of harmonious ecstasy:

> And mine in this was wound, and whirl'd
>   About empyreal heights of thought,
>   And came on that which is, and caught
> The deep pulsations of the world,

The 'Aeonian music' of the succeeding stanza suggests perhaps something permanent within the mutability of the merely and supremely human act of love. The trance ends, and the final four stanzas return the poem to its opening landscape, now perceived at dawn. This framework of landscape serves to suggest the poet's temporary absence from the ambient physical world, and it may be that the breeze which trembles through the leaves and flowers possesses genuinely pentecostal associations, like that of Eliot's *Four Quartets*. The dawn brings, after the stressful vision of the trance, an access of greater assurance and optimism for the poet, and apparently for his age:

> And East and West, without a breath,
>   Mixt their dim lights, like life and death,
> To broaden into boundless day.

## Faith and Doubt

Charles Kingsley, when he read *In Memoriam*, designated it 'the noblest Christian poem which England has produced for two centuries'. Modern criticism, placing the emphasis somewhat differently, has emphasized the poem's expressions of doubt and despair. The poem clearly debates such issues as the power of the deity, the meaning of death, the nature of nature, and the speaker's role in the scheme of things. But at bottom the poem perhaps does not demonstrate a discovery of fulfilment through the perception of a philosophical design so much as a gradually enlarging consciousness, the reading of meaning into a tragically shattered life. The construction of a personality arises through combining the past and the present. The evidence for the existence of God in the scriptures is starkly ignored throughout, and to that extent *In Memoriam* cannot be accounted a religious poem.

The work begins by examining the disjunction between the perceiving self and the past on both personal and impersonal levels. The early sections are characterized by a 'wild and wandering' utterance, and what the eye perceives is void and without sense: the 'bald street', the 'blank day' of the London poem (7) are emblematic of a deeper cognitive blankness and overwhelming absence of meaning. Nature is fragmented, and the speaker of the poem stumbles 'Upon the great world's altar-stairs/ That slope thro' darkness up to God', able only to 'stretch lame hands of faith, and grope,/ And gather dust and chaff' (55). Even the happiness of the past seems now shifting and uncertain, and Tennyson wonders whether it is the 'lowness of the present state,/ That sets the past in this relief' (24). There is no divinity, no sense of purposive development, within such experience; Eliot suggested that the poem's stature lay in the quality of its doubt, and Tennyson himself described the poem as 'too hopeful'. In places, the poem suggests that the divine is really a chimera, a reflection of a human reality:

> What find I in the highest place,
>   But mine own phantom chanting hymns?
>   And on the depths of death there swims
> The reflex of a human face.

(108)

Certainly the dead do not speak, as they are liable to do, for instance, in Yeats. Hallam's own 'immortality' appears most often to take the form of living within the memory of others – scarcely an orthodox Christian reading of the afterlife. Indeed, Tennyson's references to individual immortality are understandably vague, and at times he finds only:

> Upon the last and sharpest height,
>     Before the spirits fade away,
>     Some landing-place, to clasp and say,
> 'Farewell! We lose ourselves in light.'
>
> (47)

The process which the poem lays bare is thus a process founded upon the difficulties attendant upon emerging out of fragmented meaninglessness, a process in which a mystical apprehension of time and presence is crucial. Towards the beginning the persona of the speaker is weak, held captive by reality as the 'dreamless head' of Hallam is caught up in the fibres of the ancient yew tree (2). It is through an exertion and exercise of the will that the 'finer mind' (18) is formed, part of the very substance of the poem being the acts of training 'To riper growth the mind and will' (42). Such natural imagery is crucial to the poem's organizing principles, and this imagery effloresces in section 115 and elsewhere. There is indeed a sense, argued for in some sections, of Hallam's ashes fertilizing the land: 'from his ashes may be made/ The violet of his native land' (18). Such moments of interpenetration act as a counter to the blankness of a nature elsewhere construed as horrifically 'red in tooth and claw'. Throughout a catalogue of social and revolutionary changes, with ancient institutions crumbling as the 'red fool-fury of the Seine' piles her 'barricades with the dead', Hallam's spirit appears to suggest the seeds of something higher to which faith aspires. This notion is expressed with some complexity in section 116, which meditates upon the cost of remaking the self:

> Is it, then, regret for buried time
>     That keenlier in sweet April wakes,
>     And meets the year, and gives and takes
> The colours of the crescent prime?
>
> Not all: the songs, the stirring air,
>     The life re-orient out of dust,
>     Cry thro' the sense to hearten trust
> In that which made the world so fair.
>
> (116)

Natural and social disasters are thus transformed by the model of Hallam's life and career; the beloved is a 'dear spirit, happy star' who 'O'erlooks't the tumult from afar,/ And smilest, knowing all is well' (127).

Theories of evolutionary change get mixed up, within the poem, with Christian imagery of suffering and purgation through fire and earthquake, but these larger theological reflections are always subdued to the service of the developing persona who searches for meaning. The imaginary parliamentary example of Hallam provides the poet with a powerful insight into, and defence against, those psychic shocks of which Freud was to write:

> A life in civic action warm,
>   A soul on highest mission sent,
>   A potent voice of Parliament,
> A pillar steadfast in the storm,
>
> Should licensed boldness gather force,
>   Becoming, when the time has birth,
>   A lever to uplift the earth
> And roll it in another course,
>
> With thousand shocks that come and go,
>   With agonies, with energies,
>   With overthrowings, and with cries,
> And undulations to and fro.
>
> (113)

If Hallam does indeed represent 'The herald of a higher race' (118), that higher race will take the form of greater self-consciousness attained through spiritual growth.

The questions confronted in *In Memoriam*, Tennyson held, were universal: does man possess an immortal soul? does life have meaning? is there any discernible process in nature? The poem does not explicitly utilize the props of Christian belief in defining and explaining the shocking effects of grief upon the poet. From around the time of the second Christmas, rehabilitation through nature appears possible, a regenerative spirit most beautifully expressed and defined in the Barmouth lyric:

> Sweet after showers, ambrosial air,
>   That rollest from the gorgeous gloom
>   Of evening over brake and bloom
> And meadow, slowly breathing bare

> The round of space, and rapt below
>> Thro' all the dewy-tassell'd wood,
>> And shadowing down the hornèd flood
> In ripples, fan my brows and blow
>
> The fever from my cheek, and sigh
>> The full new life that feeds thy breath
>> Throughout my frame, till Doubt and Death,
> Ill brethren, let the fancy fly
>
> From belt to belt of crimson seas
>> On leagues of odour streaming far,
>> To where in yonder orient star
> A hundred spirits whisper 'Peace'.

(86)

The subtle articulation of poetic structure here is wedded to climatic phenomena on the Welsh coast: the clearance of the sky and the poet's spiritual liberation are expressed in a rhythm which matches and enacts the rolling away of the clouds. Such moments do not, of course, sweep away personal or religious difficulties. On the contrary, 'There lies more faith in honest doubt,/ Believe me, than in half the creeds' (96). To the argument, advanced perhaps by Emily Sellwood, that religious doubt is 'Devil-born', the poet responds with the example of Hallam himself: 'He fought his doubts.'

Science, for all its renewed potency and ambition in the nineteenth century, cannot dispel doubt or illuminate the mysteries of religion, and in section 124 Tennyson seeks finally to express what faith he has attained through suffering. The urgent promptings of the heart lie at the base of mankind:

> That which we dare invoke to bless;
>> Our dearest faith; our ghastliest doubt;
>> He, They, One, All; within, without;
> The Power in darkness whom we guess;

This 'Power' is discoverable 'not in world or sun,/ Or eagle's wing'; it is the heart which 'Stood up and answer'd "I have felt"', though that declarative bravery is quickly qualified:

> No, like a child in doubt and fear:
>> But that blind clamour made me wise;
>> Then was I as a child that cries,
> But, crying, knows his father near;

(124)

As R. H. Hutton commented in 1892, there is a crucially 'agnostic element' in Tennyson. The poet, Hutton argued, 'finds no authoritative last word such as many Christians find in ecclesiastical authority'. He went on:

The generally faltering voice with which Tennyson expresses the ardour of his own hope, touches the heart of this doubting and questioning age, as no more confident expression of belief could have touched it. The lines of his theology were in harmony with the great central lines of Christian thought; but in coming down to detail it soon passed into a region where all was wistful, and dogma disappeared in a haze of radiant twilight.

The Prologue to *In Memoriam* was a final piece of the jig-saw to be put into place, in 1849. It seems designed to demonstrate just how far Tennyson could go in acceptance of Christian doctrine:

> We have but faith: we cannot know;
> For knowledge is of things we see;
> And yet we trust it comes from thee,
> A beam in darkness: let it grow.

Henry Sidgwick complained that 'Faith, in the introduction, is too completely triumphant.' But this is a cavil which might more justly be aimed at the Epilogue, a poem which expresses the persuasively rhetorical vision of progress towards a higher life, a vision in which the faltering voice of honest doubt, for the time, is silenced in the final invocation to the deity.

## Poetry and Geology

The thesis of development and natural selection was not new to the Victorians. On the contrary, it was already a familiar element in the thought of ancient Greece. But in the period prior to the publication of Darwin's *Origin of Species* in 1859 the books which made the greatest contribution to popular debate were Sir Charles Lyell's *Principles of Geology* (1830–33) and Robert Chambers's *Vestiges of Creation* (1844), both known to the poet. Lyell rejected the theological notion of a series of catastrophes, arguing instead that 'all former changes of the organic and inorganic creation are referrable to one uninterrupted succession of physical events, governed by the laws now in operation'. One element which effected great changes, Lyell stressed, was water acting upon rocks over millennia, and this image surfaces several times in Tennyson's text. Chambers, unlike Lyell, found Lamarck's notion of evolutionary change persuasive. Lamarck, whose *Philosophie zoologique* was published in

1809, argued that God allowed natural evolution whereby simply organized creatures gave way to creatures of greater complexity. Thus all nature exhibits a fundamental ancestral unity under the law of development. Whilst Chambers regarded the arrangement of species as 'perfect', he also saw the individual as abandoned to 'take his chance amidst the mêlée of the various laws affecting him'. The evolutionary system, that is to say, 'has the fairness of a lottery, in which everyone has the like chance of drawing the prize'.

*In Memoriam* is undoubtedly, in some of its sections, generated by this evolutionary gradualism. The great length of the work allows the poet the range and scope necessary to contemplate these universal processes. The examination of states of mind, ranging from grief, through doubt, to chastened optimism goes hand in hand with, and is often expressed through, meditations upon the new scientific world-view. Personal desolation is matched with hopelessness at the random vacancy of nature, and this melancholia is gradually replaced by acceptance upon both emotional and intellectual levels within the poet.

Placing of Hallam's death within a larger pattern is paralleled with a recognition of the patterns of change in nature. At the outset the speaker inevitably desires permanence to offset his shock:

> But who shall so forecast the years
>     And find in loss a gain to match?
>     Or reach a hand thro' time to catch
> The far-off interest of tears?
>
> (1)

The pious hope that 'men may rise on stepping-stones' (1) is shattered by the fact of loss and absence in the present, to the extent that contemplation of nature becomes a nightmarish experience summed up in the words of Sorrow:

> 'The stars,' she whispers, 'blindly run;
>     A web is wov'n across the sky;
>     From out waste places comes a cry,
> And murmurs from the dying sun:'
>
> (3)

Under such a view the universe is nothing more nor less than a dead mechanism from which Tennyson feels utterly alienated, a 'dream,/ A discord' which renders life 'as futile, then, as frail' (56). The speaker of the poem is confused and baffled, and nature now reflects the private disorder within the perceiving mind. There is here little of that sacramental view of nature celebrated in Ruskin or Hopkins. The crux of these scientific doubts lies in sections 55 and 56: God and nature are apparently 'at strife', and in this strife the care taken over the 'type' or species is only matched surrealistically by the wanton carelessness over the 'single life':

> That I, considering everywhere
>   Her secret meaning in her deeds,
>   And finding that of fifty seeds
> She often brings but one to bear,
>
> I falter where I firmly trod,
>
> (55)

Indeed, it may be that nature is not even careful of the type, since so many have already vanished.

It is only through an inner conviction of the worth and value of Hallam's life, and of his friend's immortality in human memory, that Tennyson can begin to view nature somewhat more optimistically by accepting the law of continuous transmutation laid bare in Lyell, Chambers and other writers of the period. This realization, which reaches its apogee in the vision of Hallam in 95, endows the natural and spiritual worlds with a perceived harmony and regularity, and in section 123 Tennyson's poetic rendition of geological theory is couched in different terms from his earlier ruminations:

> There rolls the deep where grew the tree.
>   O earth, what changes hast thou seen!
>   There where the long street roars, hath been
> The stillness of the central sea.
>
> The hills are shadows, and they flow
>   From form to form, and nothing stands;
>   They melt like mist, the solid lands,
> Like clouds they shape themselves and go.
>
> (123)

Here the landscape is deliquescent, visionary, melting and fluid; its shifting tonality marks and expresses the instability of the perceiving persona, but that persona now has some foundations of faith with which to interpret this world of shifting traces:

> . . . They say
> The solid earth whereon we tread

> In tracts of fluent heat began,
>> And grew to seeming-random forms,
>> The seeming prey of cyclic storms,
> Till at the last arose the man;

(118)

Nature's continuous change is here pervaded by purpose and order, by a sense of process leading to the appearance of the 'herald of a higher race'. What man does today will determine the future of the species just as, in the Epilogue, Tennyson feels able to claim, 'I myself with these have grown/ To something greater than before'.

Evolutionary thought made an enormous impact upon the Victorian psyche. As Ruskin joked, 'You can't wash the slugs out of a lettuce without disrespect to your ancestors.' The theory was of crucial significance in the imaginative life of the time, and *In Memoriam* nicely captures many of the conflicting feelings and attitudes to evolution within the period. Evolution gave to the writer a number of insights which he or she could creatively utilize, notably the concept of struggle linked with man's animal past; the idea of vast stretches of time; and the alteration of fixed systems into a vision of development and 'progress'. The nodal concept of transition, of a world which was to be comprehended, in the words of Friedrich Engels, 'not as a complex of ready-made *things*, but as a complex of *processes*', radically affected the writer's sense of those previously fixed essences, 'self' and 'nature'. Evolution theory, particularly after the publication of *The Origin of Species* (1859), was enabling for writers in creating both a myth of origins and, as in *In Memoriam*, a myth of ends. The evolution theory of *In Memoriam*, as of other literary texts of the period, may be best thought of as a poetic construct or myth which fertilized the poet's imagination through a type of creative misreading of his scientific sources. As Gillian Beer remarks, in her magisterial analysis of the matter, evolution theory implied a new myth of the past, and of human life:

Instead of man, emptiness – or the empire of molluscs. There was no way back to a previous paradise: the primordial was comfortless. Instead of fixed and perfect species, it showed forms in flux, and the earth in constant motion, drawing continents apart. This consciousness of the fluent, of the physical world as endless onward process, extended to an often pained awareness of human beings as slight elements within unstoppable motion and transformation.

Tennyson's great poem illuminates and verifies Beer's observation that individualism, under the evolutionary shadow, 'is set under a new and almost intolerable tension'.[15]

## The Sexuality of *In Memoriam*

That *In Memoriam* records a love between two men is an inescapable fact of the text, but it is a fact over which criticism stumbles. The evasions of Tennyson's critics have been refreshingly challenged by Alan Sinfield,[16] and his reading of this contentious matter may help to clarify and illuminate the question for other readers. Feeling that the critical failure to deal with the sexual issues raised by *In Memoriam* is 'a scandal', he notes how much ink has been spilt upon problems of science and religion in the poem whilst 'a subversion of mainstream construction of sexuality is either explained away or, even more firmly, not discussed at all'. The direct evidence is tentative: words deleted from section 93, 'Stoop soul, and touch me: wed me' (though as Ricks remarks, the revised 'Descend, and touch, and enter' may be even more disconcerting); Benjamin Jowett's remark (erased by Hallam Tennyson) about Tennyson's 'sort of sympathy with Hellenism'; and the letter from Tennyson to his friend Spedding, who had jokingly speculated that Tennyson and Hallam slept together at Somersby, reassuring him nervously that 'we have a spare bed'. Ricks assembles this evidence, and justly suggests that 'a certain privacy limits the nature of *In Memoriam* – but it also provides some of its sources of energy'. Sinfield seeks, by challenging the notion of sexuality as a dehistoricized natural drive, to argue that sexuality is, to some extent, socially constructed. He notes, following Michel Foucault, that, contrary to popular belief, the Victorians were not sexually repressed: 'On the contrary, they thought and wrote and talked about it a great deal and turned it into the discourse to which all else can be referred.'

The relationship between Hallam and Tennyson can productively be sited within a range of homosexual experiences; it conforms to what Jeffrey Weeks, quoted by Sinfield, describes as 'the highly individualised, the deeply emotional, sometimes even sexual, relation between two individuals who are otherwise not regarded, or do not regard themselves, as "deviant"'. As Weeks observes elsewhere,[17] this kind of relationship 'avoids all the problems of commitment and identity'. Self-evidently, the relationship of which *In Memoriam* is the literary memorial was not primarily or consciously sexual in nature, but Sinfield protests against the tendency complacently to subsume the relationship within the harmlessly wide category of 'friendship': 'Such intensity of male bonding was situated ambiguously and provocatively in the complex field of nineteenth-century sexuality.' An early review of the anonymously published *In Memoriam* declared, 'these touching lines evidently come from the full heart of the widow of a military man', and Sinfield points this out as evidence of his thesis about the 'femininity' of Tennyson's art in an age of utilitarian commerce. Part of the compulsive interest in *In Memoriam* is its quality of being, as Eliot claimed, 'the concentrated diary of a man confessing himself', and this intensity is produced, Sinfield argues, through a mode which fits the stanza form into the established patterns of love poetry. Thus the Wimpole Street poem, for instance, may fruitfully be interrogated for its sexual ambivalence and intertextual coding:

> Dark house, by which once more I stand
>     Here in the long unlovely street,
>     Doors, where my heart was used to beat
> So quickly, waiting for a hand,
>
> A hand that can be clasp'd no more –
>     Behold me, for I cannot sleep,
>     And like a guilty thing I creep
> At earliest morning to the door.
>
> (7)

Sinfield remarks of this:

The classical love elegy offered itself as a discourse for Tennyson to use, but the complexities set up through its derivation from cultures where sexuality was regarded very differently, together with the interaction of that with the un-orthodoxy of Tennyson's feelings for Arthur, result in a disturbance of customary gender categories. It is not that Tennyson is revealed to have 'homosexual tend-encies' – that would enable us to pigeonhole him – but that there is no proper fit to be achieved with received discourses.

This is well put, and Sinfield proceeds to show how Tennyson legitimizes his confused feelings by calling up, in section 8, the more 'universal' analogy of heterosexual love:

> A happy lover who has come
>     To look on her that loves him well,
>     Who 'lights and rings the gateway bell,
> And learns her gone and far from home;
>
> He saddens, all the magic light
>     Dies off at once from bower and hall,
>     And all the place is dark, and all
> The chambers emptied of delight:
>
> (8)

Tennyson's project of rendering his feelings acceptable collapses, as Sinfield points out, in the black depression of the final line, 'For all is dark where thou art not' – once again the language subverts the channelling of feeling along conventionally readerly lines. Hallam is seen variously in the poem as analogous to father, mother, female beloved, deserted lady, or wife, but in each case Sinfield argues that 'there is the danger of an unattributable excess of sexual implication'. He quotes a suppressed stanza from section 97, where the marital imagery breaks out into a wild physicality:

> They madly drank each other's breath
> With breast to breast in early years.
> They met with passion and with tears,
> Their every parting was a death.

The notions of death and heaven present the poet with a range of language and imagery which he bends to his purpose in highly ambiguous ways. Through death, Hallam becomes superior to the bereft poet, who it seems may even become forgotten: whilst the poet's passionate emotion may be dismissed as an 'idle tale' and 'fading legend', Hallam is imagined moving into higher realms:

> And thou, as one that once declined,
> When he was little more than boy,
> On some unworthy heart with joy,
> But lives to wed an equal mind;
>
> And breathes a novel world, the while
> His other passion wholly dies,
> Or in the light of deeper eyes
> Is matter for a flying smile.
>
> (62)

There may well be, as Sinfield detects, a resentment against Hallam in such lines, a note which recurs in the analogy of marital coldness:

> Her life is lone, he sits apart,
> He loves her yet, she will not weep,
> Tho' rapt in matters dark and deep
> He seems to slight her simple heart.
>
> (97)

Tennyson explicated this obscure passage as being about 'the relation of one on earth to one in the other and higher world', but Sinfield suggests that there is a revealing undertone here which marks a 'superior and neglectful stance' on the part of Hallam which continues a 'pattern of relations between the two young men which was established while Arthur was alive'. Tennyson indeed wrote of himself as 'like some poor girl whose heart is set/ On one whose rank exceeds her own', and there must have been many indications, in their time at Cambridge, of the social gap between the two young men. Ideas of death and heaven enable Tennyson to obliterate this gap and to work within comforting images and responses, but they fail to contain the underlying disturbance of customary ideas about masculinity. Towards the end, Tennyson closes down these contradictions by so transmuting the death/heaven imagery as to suggest virtual identification between Hallam and Christ:

> Known and unknown; human, divine;
>   Sweet human hand and lips and eye;
>   Dear heavenly friend that canst not die,
> Mine, mine, for ever, ever mine;
>
> Strange friend, past, present, and to be;
>   Loved deeplier, darklier understood;
>   Behold, I dream a dream of good,
> And mingle all the world with thee.

(129)

The iambic tetrameter of *In Memoriam*, with its inner and outer couplet rhyming scheme, serves well to mask and smooth out dissonance and contradiction here. Early readers of the poem undoubtedly echoed the views of G. H. Lewes that sorrow had 'purified' Tennyson. The work, Lewes held, 'mingles with our life, enlarges our capacity of feeling, deepens our sympathy, converts the egotism of our nature, and raises our moral development'. Yet for the reader of *In Memoriam* today what Lewes nominated the poem's 'chastened strains' contain complex and subversive undertones issuing out of an undeclared sexual ambiguity to which Sinfield justifiably draws the reader's attention. Confusion of role and identity serve to produce a text of rich and disturbing power.

## New Readings

In recent years the somewhat comfortable (and comforting) consensus on the structure, meaning and significance of *In Memoriam* has been dislocated by new accounts of the work which seek to relate new movements in critical theory to Tennyson's multivalent text.

There is space here only to refer to two such accounts, but it is hoped that summaries of the argument will help to demonstrate the richness and excitement available to the reader who is prepared to struggle with some of the difficulties of post-structural critical writing. In an essay entitled 'Strategies of Containment: Tennyson's *In Memoriam*',[18] Rob Johnson seeks to show how the concept of *difference*, defined in general terms as 'any discrepant and potentially disruptive element in personal consciousness, in society at large and in current perceptions of the cosmos', is contained but never eradicated by the text. Through close analysis of the Prologue, with its resounding invocation to the 'Son of God, immortal love', Johnson tries to show that the argument for God's existence and man's immortality is made to seem, through the double-edged nature of the rhetoric, 'distinctly precarious'. He remarks interestingly on the contrastive use of 'think/know' in the Prologue, a duality which brings an overtone of 'anxiety in what is, logically speaking, a positive argument'. The rhetorical marshalling of positive arguments for immortality possesses, therefore, a dark underside which is an inescapable aspect of all meaning, since language is not a fixed system of signifiers. The key to this type of reading is the notion of *play*: the 'play of signifiers' prevents any final and definitive reading of the Prologue (or indeed of the poem as a whole). What the text produces in the reader is a variety of possible readings each of which challenges or 'deconstructs' the other in a permanent postponement of any finally determined reading. There are, Johnson concedes, different readings possible, but he warns that 'any reading for which we settle will be haunted by our awareness of others'. It is through such reading (or misreading) that we may construct the 'haunted consciousness' of the speaker of the poem.

In the first phase of *In Memoriam* the speaker is 'too disorientated by grief to be capable of reading himself at all'. The self or subject is 'divided between the "I" that is puzzled and the "I" that puzzles':

> O heart, how fares it with thee now,
> That thou should'st fail from thy desire,
> Who scarcely darest to inquire,
> 'What is it makes me beat so low?'

(4)

Tennyson himself remarked that, in the poem, ' "I" is not always the author speaking of himself', and Johnson argues that in the first parts of the poem the 'I' 'is not a coherent fictive presence'. He refers specifically to the section in which the ship carrying Hallam's body arrives in England and a living Hallam steps on shore:

> And if along with these should come
>     The man I held as half-divine;
>     Should strike a sudden hand in mine,
> And ask a thousand things of home; . . .
>
> And I perceived no touch of change,
>     No hint of death in all his frame,
>     But found him all in all the same,
> I should not feel it to be strange.
>
> (14)

In the final line, as Johnson observes, the 'I' of the poem's narrative is 'scrutinised by an implicit other "I" who finds it strange that the first "I" finds nothing strange'. Thus the notion of the 'speaker' of *In Memoriam* is problematized; he is 'a stranger to himself, baffled by his own behaviour':

> What words are these have fall'n from me?
>     Can calm despair and wild unrest
>     Be tenants of a single breast,
> Or sorrow such a changeling be?
>
> (16)

The play of difference within language, that is to say, accentuates the uncertainties so dreadfully evident in the fact of Hallam's death. Such verbal slippage is nicely demonstrated in the calm and peaceful Lincolnshire landscape of section 11. This poem appears to draw upon pastoral and elegiac tradition, but it does so only to subvert traditional expectations. Thus the suggestion of a correlation between the calmness of nature and a calm in the perceiving mind is evoked only to be dismantled:

> Calm and deep peace in this wide air,
>     These leaves that redden to the fall;
>     And in my heart, if calm at all,
> If any calm, a calm despair:
>
> (11)

The very calmness of nature, Johnson holds, is relativized, and the calmness, if any, within the speaker is crucially differentiated from the calm of the natural world. He goes on:

The notion of a spiritual affinity with nature is further parodied in another studiedly incongruous comparison between the calm (in motion) of the sea and the 'dead calm' in the corpse's breast, 'which heaves but with the heaving deep'.

The consciousness of the speaker is fluid, and it is therefore no surprise that the verbal terms for reporting this consciousness are equally slippery. The notion of 'faith', such a crucial signifier in the poem, is shown to possess 'no consistent or precise reference', although the poem culminates in a resounding celebration of oneness and faith in its conclusion. Here difference is cancelled, and 'change contained as progress', but such a mystical union is impossible elsewhere, because the self is 'initially defined by difference', as section 45 explains:

> The baby new to earth and sky,
>   What time his tender palm is prest
>   Against the circle of the breast,
> Has never thought that 'this is I:'
>
> But as he grows he gathers much,
>   And learns the use of 'I', and 'me',
>   And finds 'I am not what I see,
> And other than the things I touch.'

(45)

The crucial 'difference' in the poem, of course, is that between the living speaker and the dead Hallam; but Johnson argues that difference 'also characterised their relationship in life': 'his unlikeness fitted mine', reflects the speaker (79), allowing difference to enrich, rather than rupture their relationship. The value of difference is explained in this section, addressed to Charles Tennyson: the speaker and his brother belong to the same 'currency', but Hallam to a foreign coinage. Through this metaphor the disruptive potency of difference has been successfully contained. Such a strategy of containment also informs the sections where the speaker is about to lose the childhood home at Somersby. He is split between 'two spirits of a diverse love' – love for the home of childhood memory and love for the place now intimately bound up with thoughts of Hallam. Yet the two, as he leaves, merge into 'one pure image of regret' (102). Home throughout the poem is a locus of oneness and unanimity, a place where the cosmic differences so sharply registered in the evolutionary sections are (temporarily) cancelled or erased. This erasure works massively, Johnson suggests, in the Epilogue, in order to produce a unified text of hope and forward-looking progress. Yet difference is 'never conclusively banished' from the text, since 'imagination remains susceptible to the dream that faith rejects'.

In another essay of considerable complexity, 'An Art that will not abandon the Self to Language',[19] Ann Wordsworth brings to bear the theoretical implications of the work of the American critic Harold Bloom upon Tennyson's poem. Bloom sees the function of a poetic tradition as a type of Oedipal struggle between the belated new poet and the powerful voice(s) of his precursor(s). The precursor is a 'strong' poet whose authority must be massively resisted in the discovery of an authentic poetic 'voice'. Poetry is produced, therefore, out of the 'anxiety of influence' and creative misprision of the father/precursor of poetic tradition. Consideration of Bloom's position leads Ann Wordsworth to consider the contrasts in readings of Tennyson between a liberal humanist critique (such as Ricks's) and an 'antithetical critique' (such as Bloom's). She notes how Ricks considers the closing lines of 'Ulysses' as marking a 'dying fall' which expresses in poetic terms his mourning over Hallam;

> . . . that which we are, we are;
> One equal temper of heroic hearts,
> Made weak by time and fate, but strong in will
> To strive, to seek, to find, and not to yield.

The key to Ricks's interpretation, Ann Wordsworth argues, 'is the psychologising of the poem so that it matches Tennyson's experiences'. Bloom, on the other hand, reads 'Ulysses' as a 'temporal victory over Milton', whose Satan had boasted his determination 'never to submit or yield'. In such a reading linguistic play is never pinned to the poet's lived experience but always to 'his struggle with earlier figurations': the poem is produced through its baffled relationship with other poems. Yet, paradoxically, it is possible for Wordsworth to claim that Bloom's reading is more psychologically valid than Ricks's biographical approach. Ricks reads 'Ulysses', and such related texts as 'Morte d'Arthur', as primarily poetic expressions of grief at the death of Hallam, expressions of mourning. Ann Wordsworth remarks, however, that the Freudian theory of mourning is a rather tougher proposition than these humanist prescriptions would allow:

According to Freud, the work of mourning is to force the ego into a testing of reality which will prove that the beloved no longer exists and that therefore all libido must be withdrawn from the dead and reinvested. This process is so painful that a moving away from reality can ensue, allowing the ego to cling to its lost object through 'hallucinatory wish psychoses'.

Bloom reads the poems prompted by the death of Hallam as 'deflections of grief into (psychotic) triumph'.

## In Memoriam A.H.H. (1850)

*In Memoriam* can be rendered safely orthodox if read as a poem of faith and doubt, but Bloom is critical of such a humanist consensus:

One never ceases to be puzzled that *In Memoriam*, an outrageously personal poem of Romantic apotheosis, a poem indeed of mostly eccentric myth-making, should have been accepted as a work of consolation and moral resolution in the tradition of Christian humanism.

As Ann Wordsworth comments drily, it is Christian/humanist literary readings which have served to render the poem 'unacceptably dull' for some readers. Such a treatment, she claims, stressing science, religion and the poet's personal experience, amounts to a kind of 'censorship' which protects the reader from the subversive or unorthodox aspects of the work and prevents critics from 'noticing that arguments about faith and doubt give way readily enough to an erotic and narcissistic triumph over death and belatedness in large sections of the poem'. The humanist impulse leads to an imposition of unity upon the recalcitrant text, but such an imposition is possible only through a wilful failure to read correctly what Bloom designates the 'bursts of radiance against a commonplace conceptual background that cannot accommodate such radiance'. The text, that is to say, resists any well-meaning effort at closure. What Ann Wordsworth designates the 'biologistic fairy tale' of the Epilogue stands thus exposed as clear proof of the coexistence of incompatible modes within the body of the poem:

rhetorical, uncanny, antithetical on the one hand, achieving an immortality forced from death by the narcissistic energies of creativity and desire; and referential, narrative and idealistic on the other, asserting a humanist optimism sealed by the pseudo-scientific notion of Hallam's reincarnation as Cecilia's unborn son.

When read thus, *In Memoriam* is undoubtedly a richer and more puzzling text, its variety and unevenness appearing as the linguistic expression of psychic turmoil. The poem, that is to say, takes the form of a massive project of exploring those confusions over loss, dereliction and immortality which energized the poet into the troubling act of writing:

> For tho' my nature rarely yields
>   To that vague fear implied in death;
>   Nor shudders at the gulfs beneath,
> The howlings from forgotten fields;
>
> Yet oft when sundown skirts the moor
>   An inner trouble I behold,
>   A spectral doubt which makes me cold,
> That I shall be thy mate no more,

> Tho' following with an upward mind
>> The wonders that have come to thee,
>> Thro' all the secular to-be,
> But evermore a life behind.

(41)

# 9. *Maud* (1855)

*Maud* owes its inception, like 'Locksley Hall', to strands of Tennyson's biography. The unbalanced state of the narrator's father which led to his suicide after speculative failures owes much to the example of Tennyson's father, and to Tennyson's own losses in Dr Allen's ill-fated woodworking project. The class distinction which separates Maud from the hero reflects the poet's imbroglio with Rosa Baring of Harrington Hall in the 1830s. Maud's father may owe something to Tennyson's grandfather, The Old Man of the Wolds, and the 'new-made Lord' with his 'gewgaw castle' casts a sly glance at Charles Tennyson d'Eyncourt and the erection and embellishment of Bayons Manor. The setting was provided by Farringford, the Tennysons' home in the Isle of Wight. Subtitling the poem a 'Monodrama', Tennyson described it as:

the history of a morbid, poetic soul, under the blighting influence of a recklessly speculative age. He is the heir of madness, an egotist with the makings of a cynic, raised to sanity by a pure and holy love which elevates his whole nature, passing from the height of triumph to the lowest depth of misery, driven into madness by the loss of her whom he has loved, and, when he has at length passed through the fiery furnace, and has recovered his reason, giving himself up to work for the good of mankind through the unselfishness of his great passion.

This account raises a number of questions, and the reader of *Maud* would do well to heed D. H. Lawrence's instruction to 'trust the tale, not the teller'. Certainly, the poet's claim that the work was 'a little *Hamlet*' is obfuscating if taken literally, though its generalized concern with the rottenness of the state clearly issues from the same world-view as that which motivated the political poems and 'Locksley Hall'. The poem is imbued with a sense of human nature acting within a natural setting which is 'one with rapine', where the 'Mayfly is torn by the swallow, the sparrow speared by the shrike'. In a world of intense economic and class struggle we find the 'heart of the citizen hissing in war on his own hearthstone', and village society dominated by the old lord, the 'gray old wolf' who has 'Dropt off gorged from a scheme that had left us flaccid and drained'. Such commercial infighting, with its concomitant survival of the fittest, has left the protagonist's father 'Mangled, and flattened, and crushed' in the 'dreadful hollow' around which the action hypnotically circles. Indeed, the social perspective is almost hysterically alarming:

> And the vitriol madness flushes up in the ruffian's head,
> Till the filthy by-lane rings to the yell of the trampled wife,
> And chalk and alum and plaster are sold to the poor for bread,
> And the spirit of murder works in the very means of life,
>
> (I, 1)

What Tennyson designated 'the blighting influence of a recklessly speculative age' extends throughout the classes, and the village becomes, metonymically, the nation at large:

> Below me, there, is the village, and looks how quiet and small!
> And yet bubbles o'er like a city, with gossip, scandal, and spite;
> And Jack on his ale-house bench has as many lies as a Czar;
> And here on the landward side, by a red rock, glimmers the Hall;
> And up in the high Hall-garden I see her pass like a light;
> But sorrow seize me if ever that light be my leading star!
>
> (I, 4)

The protagonist is 'At war with [himself]', connecting 'a time so sordid and mean' with 'myself so languid and base'. There is indifference here to the wider movements of nineteenth-century history: 'Shall I weep if a Poland fall? shall I shriek if a Hungary fail?', an indifference justified through the Thackerayan reflection that 'We are puppets . . . moved by an unseen hand at a game'. The hero lives, not unlike Mariana, 'alone in an empty house', but this emptiness is temporarily filled, absence made into full presence, by the arrival of Maud. She is at first dismissed as cold and distant, then love significantly arises through the agency of her song:

> A voice by the cedar tree
> In the meadow under the Hall!
> She is singing an air that is known to me,
> A passionate ballad gallant and gay,
> A martial song like a trumpet's call!
>
> (I, 5)

This call to action leads to a potentially redemptive pattern of life through a cult of leadership and 'masculinity':

> Ah God, for a man with heart, head, hand,
> Like some of the simple great ones gone
> For ever and ever by,

> One still strong man in a blatant land,
> Whatever they call him, what care I,
> Aristocrat, democrat, autocrat – one
> Who can rule and dare not lie.
>
> (I, 10)

The firmness of will so shrilly signalled here is radically undone by the killing of Maud's brother, and the heroine's subsequent death from grief. The remainder of the poem allows Maud to exist only within the narrator's disintegrating consciousness, one set of memories of her being suspicious and petty-minded and the other, contradictory set turning the hero's face towards a doctrine of direct heroic action. At the close the protagonist departs for the 'blood-red blossoms with a heart of fire', mixing his breath 'with a loyal people shouting a battle cry'.

Tennyson once told his friend James Knowles, 'No other poem (a monotone with plenty of change and no weariness) has been made into a drama where successive phases of passion in one person take the place of successive persons.' Certainly the problematic pleasures of reading *Maud* are focused upon this creation of a *speaker*: the hero is divided against himself, like the nation in which he lives so miserably, and that self-division is enacted in the text by the widely different stanza forms which Tennyson deploys. As Ricks well observes, 'Tennyson's lack of certain kinds of dramatic gift focussed his mind and heart upon that tension between stasis and outcome which the dramatic monologue was uniquely fitted to explore and interpret.' The self-imposed prison of mania is subtly explored in the relationship with the beloved. Maud is at first perceived as a cold and distant vision:

> . . . she has neither savour nor salt,
> But a cold and clear-cut face, as I found when her carriage past,
> Perfectly beautiful: let it be granted her: where is the fault?
> All that I saw (for her eyes were downcast, not to be seen)
> Faultily faultless, icily regular, splendidly null,
> Dead perfection, no more;
>
> (I, 2)

Indeed, there is a kind of horror at the demands of love which the poem circles around, a hatred subliminally foreshadowed in the dramatic opening evocation of the hollow, a place whose 'surrealistic' quality, Ricks remarks, 'suggests a bleeding woman':

> I hate the dreadful hollow behind the little wood,
> Its lips in the field above are dabbled with blood-red heath,

> The red-ribb'd ledges drip with a silent horror of blood,
> And Echo there, whatever is ask'd her, answers 'Death'.

(I, 1)

The violently eroticized scenery with which Tennyson begins his poem bears out Freud's argument that 'the complicated topography of the female genital parts makes one understand how it is that they are often represented as landscapes'. The death of the father suggests an Oedipal wish-fulfilment and a feral distaste for the reality of the female body which will mark both hero and text. In an interesting discussion of the matter,[20] Jonathan Wordsworth addresses the question of how consciously Tennyson is here utilizing sexual symbolism. The matter of the poem – the father's suicide, the desired death of the guilty man, the love for his daughter, and the death of his son – reads differently, as Wordsworth remarks, to a post-Freudian age. If one begins to read these opening lines in terms of the female body, 'the surface level of Tennyson's narrative abruptly disappears'. As that happens 'one understands the intensity of the hatred because one sees that in the narrator's fantasy, sex – the act of giving *him* life – has brought about his father's death'. The sexually explicit imagery of the 'Come into the garden Maud' sequence is violently juxtaposed with the opening of Part II:

> 'The fault was mine, the fault was mine' –
> Why am I sitting here so stunn'd and still,
> Plucking the harmless wild-flower on the hill? –
> It is this guilty hand!

(II, 1)

Of this juxtaposition Jonathan Wordsworth observes, 'If Tennyson saw no rhyme implied, no hint that the plucking was a deflowering (that led to the passionate cry, and the blood on the lips) we are bound to do.' The duel returns the action to the hollow, the originary space of the action which is both womb-like and sexual, and Wordsworth argues from this that the action is symbolic of adult lovemaking, an activity which the neurotic narrator simply cannot accept or cope with.

*Maud* is very much a poem of extremity. The hero connects masculinity with both aggression and corruption: a male-dominated utilitarian system is contrasted with the figure of woman as the Other, carrier of associations of civility, peace and beauty. The men in the poem, as viewed by the speaker, are corrupt; the women (and himself) pure. But the incorporation of himself among the women leads the hero into impossible contradictions: 'At war with myself and a wretched race,/ Sick, sick to the heart of life, am I'. The primary impulse of the early sections is to announce the hero's separation from all human society, a separation marked by his attacking all things masculine and elevating all things female. When he encounters Maud he endeavours to make these fantasies real and exposes himself to the very society he disdains, uncovering unresolvable complexities in human relations: Maud's brother, it turns out, is capable of both aggression and tenderness, Maud a beautiful singer of warlike ballads.

The poem begins therefore in a cynical frame of mind. The narrator is bereft of any real sense of self through the death of his father, and is consequently unable to frame any mature moral evaluation:

> Villainy somewhere! whose? One says, we are villains all.
> Not he: his honest fame should at least by me be maintained:
> But that old man, now lord of the broad estate and the Hall,
> Dropt off gorged from a scheme that had left us flaccid and drain'd.
>
> (I, 1)

There is 'villainy somewhere', though it is not to be located in himself or his dead father, and the interdependent nature of good and evil is part of the meaning of the poem. The denunciations of contemporary society are feverish and shrill, evidently the product of an unbalanced mind:

> Peace sitting under her olive, and slurring the days gone by,
> When the poor are hovell'd and hustled together, each sex, like swine,
> When only the ledger lives, and when only not all men lie;
> Peace in her vineyard – yes! – but a company forges the wine.
>
> (I, 1)

Are we meant to read such vituperation as genuinely felt protest at the world's ills, or as emanating from a diseased mind? Certainly in the present state of society war is envisaged as a purifying process which will end the commercial competition of peacetime. The outbreak of hostilities, the hero believes, would effect the spiritual awakening of the nation, and even of the pusillanimous tradesmen: 'the smooth-faced snubnosed rogue would leap from his counter and till,/ And strike, if he could, were it but with his cheating yardwand, home'. The state, overtly at war with itself, will unite in the face of a foreign enemy, and such warmongering serves nicely to mask the vacillating nature of the speaker, immersed in his private woes. Even before he catches sight of Maud, the hero suggests that she 'may bring [him] a curse', and he reaches a satisfyingly dismissive conclusion after his first glimpse of her aristocratic features. But this posture cannot be sustained after the vision of section five:

> Maud with her exquisite face,
> And wild voice pealing up to the sunny sky,
> And feet like sunny gems on an English green,
> Maud in the light of her youth and her grace,
> Singing of Death, and of Honour that cannot die,
> Till I well could weep for a time so sordid and mean,
> And myself so languid and base.
>
> (I, 5)

Under this influence the narrator is warmed back to a kind of life which helps him to transcend his earlier Darwinian vision of a nature 'one with rapine'. Maud's battle-song speaks to something deep within the protagonist's consciousness. Her face is matched by her 'wild voice' as she sings of 'Death, and of Honour', 'in the light of her youth and her grace'. Recognition of Maud and her song leads to recognition of a deeper complexity and emotional warmth:

> If Maud were all that she seem'd,
> And her smile were all that I dream'd,
> Then the world were not so bitter
> But a smile could make it sweet.
>
> (I, 6)

But the developing attraction is characterized by a competing male presence, that of Maud's brother: 'I met her today with her brother, but not to her brother I bowed'. The hero keeps aloof from this 'Assyrian Bull' of a brother, clearly perturbed by the latter's animalism and masculine energy, childishly persuading himself that the brother has inherited the evil of the father whilst Maud is 'only the child of her mother'. This idealization of the beloved, so typical of much Victorian art and poetry, possesses a cloying sickliness, which later prompted Edgell Rickwood, in his Great War poem, 'Trench Poets', ironically to describe the rotting body of his dead companion thus:

> There was one thing that I might do
> to starve the worms; I racked my head
> for healthy things and quoted *Maud.*
> His grin got worse and I could see
> He sneered at passion's purity.
> He stank so badly, though we were great chums
> I had to leave him; then rats ate his thumbs.

The invented jealousy with the 'new-made lord' riding out with Maud is in reality a protection of the self:

> Seeing his gewgaw castle shine,
> New as his title, built last year,
> There amid perky larches and pine,
> And over the sullen-purple moor
> (Look at it) pricking a cockney ear.

(I, 10)

This animus against the industrial nouveau riche links up, curiously in his distempered mind, with an attack on the peace-monger, a 'broad-brimmed hawker of holy things' stained by the collusion between money and manufacture.

But the growing obsession with Maud gives the hero reason to believe that love can bring unity to the world and give his own shiftless personality a solid ground of being: 'O let the solid ground/ Not fail beneath my feet', he cries. Nature itself seems capable of renewal, in an access of the romantic imagination, but this is once again a case of a projection of the 'self'. Rather than mingling with the world and participating in it, it is as if the hero were talking to himself: Maud is to be 'Mine, mine by right, from birth till death' – like Golding's Pincher Martin, Tennyson's protagonist devours what he loves. The fantasy of possession leads into some of the most remarkable passages of the poem, where the heroine is imagined in terms of an Edenic garden imagery created in a deliberately tripping rhythm:

> Maud has a garden of roses
> And lilies fair on a lawn;
> There she walks in her state
> And tends upon bed and bower,
> And thither I climb'd at dawn
> And stood by her garden-gate;
> A lion ramps at the top,
> He is claspt by a passion-flower.

(I, 14)

The curiously erotic conjunction here of bed, ramping lion and passion-flower leads directly into the climactic 'Come into the garden, Maud', but this ecstatic strain is proleptically undermined by the magnificent episode where the hero gazes at the great house in the dawn light:

> I heard no sound where I stood
> But the rivulet on from the lawn
> Running down to my own dark wood;

> Or the voice of the long sea-wave as it swell'd
> Now and then in the dim-gray dawn;
> But I look'd, and round, all round the house I beheld
> The death-white curtain drawn;
> Felt a horror over me creep,
> Prickle my skin and catch my breath,
> Knew that the death-white curtain meant but sleep,
> Yet I shudder'd and thought like a fool of the sleep of death.
>
> (I, 14)

The conventional iconography of the lover outside the beloved's dwelling is given an authentic Tennysonian *frisson* of despair and horror. The sounds – the babbling rivulet and the 'voice' of the sea-wave – give place to the preternatural silence of the shuttered house, the life-flow of nature becoming embalmed in the corpse-like emblematic building, whose appearance is misread by the perceiving eye. There is here that desire to fix Maud into the stasis of death which the hero's morbidly egocentric passion will finally accomplish, so that the ensuing joy of 'Go not, happy day', with its primary metaphor of the sexual blush, feels curiously misplaced. Maud is seen as a possession, and her docility taken for granted:

> I have led her home, my love, my only friend.
> There is none like her, none.
> And never yet so warmly ran my blood
> And sweetly, on and on
> Calming itself to the long-wish'd-for end,
> Full to the banks, close on the promised good.
>
> (I, 18)

The brother's return interrupts this fantasy of possession and engulfment. At the climax of the love passages Maud urges the hero to accept her brother. She:

> . . . wishes me to approve him,
> And tells me, when she lay
> Sick once, with a fear of worse,
> That he left his wine and horses and play,
> Sat with her, read to her, night and day,
> And tended her like a nurse.
>
> (I, 19)

The brother's mixed humanity challenges the stereotype created in the protagonist's fevered brain. The hero tries to obliterate his jealousy, but the imagery of burial is only too revealing:

> So now I have sworn to bury
> All this dead body of hate,
> I feel so free and so clear
> By the loss of that dead weight,

(I, 19)

'Come into the garden, Maud', brilliantly composed to mime the rhythm of the polka, marks both the fulfilment of his love and the permanent separation from life which characterizes the hero's situation. Standing 'here at the gate alone' the *déclassé* hero urges the heroine to leave the vitality and life of the ball, claiming that 'She is weary of dance and play'. What he offers her in its place appears to be an engulfing fantasy of possession, fired by jealousy of his rival:

> O young lord-lover, what sighs are those,
>      For one that will never be thine?

(I, 22)

In the gap between Parts I and II the duel has occurred: it is the crucially absent action around which the inaction of the hero is organized, just as Chekhov was to structure the stagnation of late Tsarist Russia around the off-stage duel in *Three Sisters*. The brother has died aristocratically by taking the blame for the duel upon himself, and abandoning the hero to the terrors of hell:

> For front to front in an hour we stood,
> And a million horrible bellowing echoes broke
> From the red-ribb'd hollow behind the wood,
> And thunder'd up into Heaven the Christless code,
> That must have life for a blow.

(II, 1)

The empty shell which the protagonist contemplates so movingly on the coast of Brittany acts as a symbol of his own desired destruction and renewal in the ocean of life. Tennyson commented that 'the shell undestroyed amid the storm perhaps symbolises to him his own first and highest nature preserved amid the storms of passion.' But the shell also suggests the beautiful inner strength of that nature which he has earlier dismissed for its aggressive terror. Observation of the shell leads the protagonist to think of the lock of maternal hair which Maud's brother kept in his ring, and he begins to meditate on the blighted waste of his past

life. The germ of the whole poem, 'O that 'twere possible', expresses
ultimate loss after the realization that Maud herself is indeed also dead.
Losing his reason, he longs for and rejoices in a living death, immolation
and burial in a powerful passage whose rhythm acts out a blank obliteration of meaning in its reworking of the motif of the 'dreadful hollow':

> Dead, long dead,
> Long dead!
> And my heart is a handful of dust,
> And the wheels go over my head,
> And my bones are shaken with pain,
> For into a shallow grave they are thrust,
> Only a yard beneath the street,
> And the hoofs of the horses beat, beat,
> The hoofs of the horses beat,
> Beat into my scalp and my brain,

> (II, 5)

From this Poe-like entombment of the self, Part III brusquely provides
the episode of the Crimean War as the solution for the hero's difficulties.
It may be argued that in entering the fray the protagonist has simply
exchanged self-destruction for the destruction of others. In this reading,
the hero's neurosis is never cured; but the intended stress of meaning is
clearly indicative of the fact that the hero's neurosis *is* resolved through
an ennobling military conflict. The mean commercial civil war which has
dominated the years of peace is transformed into a unifying national
mission. The hero, finally emerging from the prison of selfhood, accepts
the war with heroic ardour, feeling that the citizens of Britain are finally
united in a common and transcendental purpose:

> I have felt with my native land, I am one with my kind,
> I embrace the purpose of God, and the doom assign'd.

> (III, 6)

*Maud* is a work which it is difficult to grasp as a unified text, and
some of the difficulty stems from the arbitrary nature of this conclusion.
It can of course be observed that the nineteenth century was predomi-
nantly an era of peace, and that such war-mongering sentiments read
very differently to the twentieth-century reader. A vigorous defence of
the procedures of the poem has been mounted by John Killham,[21] in an
analysis of the text which stresses the way the conclusion is 'carefully
prepared for throughout the poem'. From the opening declaration of
shock at the death of the hero's father in the 'dreadful hollow', the poem

shows how both man and nature are dominated by civil war in a universe where even the stars act tyrannically:

> Innumerable, pitiless, passionless eyes,
> Cold fires, yet with power to burn and brand
> His nothingness into man.

(I, 18)

There is little wonder, Killham argues, that the protagonist seeks to withdraw:

He is cowed by life and regrets that he ever came to possess the consciousness which causes him to believe that life involves an unremitting resort to either violence or cunning, the struggle inevitably culminating in death.

The suppression of Poland and Hungary by Russia and Austria in the late 1840s informs this desire for withdrawal, Killham believes, since international politics are seen to be dominated by 'the same ruthless pattern of violence'. Maud's military song highlights the baseness of the age, and as the hero's reasons for living increase he begins to see that death is not to be feared, but that the good may have to be defended by force:

> . . . for sullen-seeming Death may give
> More life to Love than ever is or ever was
> In our low world, where yet 'tis sweet to live.

(I, 18)

After the duel, the hero sees that violence is never justified in the personal realm, but may be required in the defence of the public good:

> Friend, to be struck by the public foe,
> Then to strike him and lay him low,
> That were a public merit, far,
> Whatever the Quaker holds, from sin;
> But the red life spilt for a private blow –
> I swear to you, lawful and lawless war
>     Are scarcely even akin.

(II, 5)

This leads on naturally, in Killham's reading, to the adoption of 'a cause that I felt to be pure and true' in Part III. A 'rigidly historical attitude' to the evils of the Crimean campaign, Killham urges, is inappropriate here. What the poem mobilizes is the notion of 'a psychic balance in man, who is obliged to accept that violence and death have to be faced as part of his lot on earth', a balance attainable through the experience of mature sexual love. It is through the range of imagery that the character's changing moods are discernible to the reader, and Killham goes on to a detailed account of the image patterns of the poem. He stresses the 'highly artificial' nature of this imagery, and sees this as signalling the 'over-brilliant, exaggeratedly alive' sensory world of the hysterical hero:

The smallest sounds are magnified by his outraged consciousness into torturing cacophony. The shriek of a mouse in the wainscot, a clock's ticking, the scream of a maddened beach [sic], the 'grinding of villainous centre-bits', are all parts of a living nightmare, in which hallucination is made to play an additional part.

Whilst readers of *Maud* would do well to study Killham's full and sympathetic treatment of the image patterns in the poem, it is also important to keep in mind the powerful exploitation in this work of the conventions of the dramatic monologue form. Quite clearly the speaker, the 'I' of the enunciation, is represented in the text, *his* text, as not wholly in control of his sanity, and the poet is painstaking in his handling of the violent tone and wild fluctuations of feeling and poetic structure in Parts I and III. The complexities of Part I arise out of a perception by the reader of both the hysteria and one-sidedness of the speaker, and also the apparent justness of the critique of Victorian commercialism. This balancing act leads to an inevitable sense of strain in the text.

The evocation of Maud herself is a nice instance of Tennyson's skill in mimetically conjuring up an unstable state of mind, with its winding sentence structure and additive clauses:

> Cold and clear-cut face, why come you so cruelly meek
> Breaking a slumber in which all spleenful folly was drown'd,
> Pale with the golden beam of an eyelash dead on the cheek,
> Passionless, pale, cold face, star-sweet on a gloom profound;
> Womanlike, taking revenge too deep for a transient wrong
> Done but in thought to your beauty, and ever as pale as before
> Growing and fading and growing upon me without a sound,
> Luminous, gemlike, ghostlike, deathlike, half the night long
> Growing and fading and growing, till I could bear it no more,
>
> (I, 3)

It is Maud's martial song which begins the newly redemptive movement, but the tone and language of the poem veer somewhat alarmingly in the treatment of the subsequent material. There is no originary centre to the discourse, only a highly 'decentred' subject capable of wild vacillation, and this instability sometimes threatens the text's discourse, betraying it into an embarrassed and banal senti- mentality:

> Dear heart, I feel with thee the drowsy spell.
> My bride to be, my evermore delight,
> My own heart's heart, my ownest own, farewell;

(I, 18)

The delicate balance between a hardly-won sanity and the ecstasy of sexual love is not always held in focus, but this difficulty does enable Tennyson to write in an ambiguous mode which can simultaneously suggest sanity and insanity, as in the diagnosis of social ills in Part II:

> Prophet, curse me the blabbing lip,
> And curse me the British vermin, the rat;
> I know not whether he came in the Hanover ship,
> But I know that he lies and listens mute
> In ancient mansion's crannies and holes;
> Arsenic, arsenic, sure, would do it,
> Except that now we poison our babes, poor souls!
> It is all used up for that.

(II, 5)

The use of the Crimean War as the solution to the hero's and the nation's problems is always likely to prove a stumbling block to the reader who has lived in the century of 'total war'. The speech and rhythm here are vigorous and unmistakable: the values of peace are denigrated in the raising of the hero's spirits and the martial increase in the rhythm:

> And it was but a dream, yet it lighten'd my despair
> When I thought that a war would arise in defence of the right,
> That an iron tyranny now should bend or cease,

(III, 6)

The rose imagery stressed by John Killham as contributing so crucially in the creation of Maud is now dangerously transformed:

> For the peace, that I deem'd no peace, is over and done,
> And now by the side of the Black and the Baltic deep,
> And deathful-grinning mouths of the fortress, flames
> The blood-red blossom of war with a heart of fire.

(III, 6)

The dangerous attractiveness of that 'blood-red blossom' has evaporated for the reader of Owen, Sassoon or Rosenberg.

There are some inventive defences of the ending of *Maud*,[22] but in the end it is hard to dissent from Sinfield's argument that here and in other later texts, Tennyson 'had trouble reading his readers and could not fix the relationship between them and himself'. The divided subject of the poem thus corresponds to divisions in the poet's personality and project. Tennyson, having finally gained the laureateship and a settled married life, perhaps felt trapped and ill at ease, constrained by his new 'public' role. *Maud*, Sinfield suggests, 'is the product of a writer who understands the game and resents it'. The problematic issue of 'manliness' seems to Sinfield the root of those incoherences of tone so characteristic of *Maud*, so that the notion of war may be read as a way through these problems, enabling a weak and 'feminized' individual boastfully to discover a kind of 'heterosexual' identity. Paradoxically, as Sinfield shows, Tennyson *did* indeed wish to offer a critique of capitalism, but because he could forge no truly radical analytical tool he took refuge in the bellicose rhetoric of the Crimean campaign. Because war is simply an extension of the capitalist struggle at home, Tennyson can only strike out angrily, predicting a consummation both feared and desired:

> Let it flame or fade, and the war roll down like a wind,
> We have proved we have hearts in a cause, we are noble still,
> And myself have awaked, as it seems, to the better mind;
>
> (III, 6)

With a view particularly to Tennyson's declining powers and increasing productiveness in his later years, the obsession with death in *Maud* may be read as signalling a kind of death of the imagination. The art of speaking, for the hero, or of writing, for the poet, is in a sense a warding-off of death. The literary work, in Michel Foucault's words, 'which once had the duty of providing immortality, now possesses the right to kill, to be its author's murderer'. The relation between writing and death in a work like *Maud* is, to borrow Foucault's argument, 'manifested in the effacement of the writing subject's individual characteristics':

Using all the contrivances that he sets up between himself and what he writes, the writing subject cancels out the signs of his particular individuality. As a result, the mark of the writer is reduced to nothing more than the singularity of his absence; he must assume the role of the dead man in the game of writing.[23]

# 10. Later Poems

## 'Enoch Arden' (1864)

By 1864 Tennyson was famous: the 1842 *Poems* and *In Memoriam* had
been followed by the embroidered tapestries of the first series of *Idylls of
the King*, in 1859. 'Enoch Arden' was an instant best-seller, though it has
since fallen from critical favour.[24] In 1859 Thomas Woolner told the
Tennysons a story he had heard, set in a fishing village, and he later tried
to persuade Tennyson to versify the tale. The poet finally agreed to do so
in 1862. Behind the story hover the shadows of Crabbe and Mrs Gaskell,
whilst the central irony of the situation seems almost to anticipate Hardy.
The narrative is recounted after the event, and generally the text main-
tains, as Ricks remarks, an 'equivocal relationship to narrative as such'.
The story is carefully plotted. In the first phase we follow the characters
from childhood to marriage, and this section culminates in Philip's dis-
appointment at losing his beloved Annie to Enoch Arden; the second
phase, commencing with Enoch's financial misfortunes, leads to his
voyage on the China-bound merchant ship, and his shipwreck on the
desert island; in the third phase he is rescued, and returns to his native
village after many years to discover Annie and Philip happily married.
Enoch finds work anonymously in the port, and finally dies, having
divulged his identity only to the publican widow, Miriam Lane. He is
given a splendid funeral by the villagers.

This story is handled by the poet primarily, it seems, with an eye to its
picturesque possibilities. The opening scene on the beach, for instance, is
proleptically organized to foretell future developments:

> And Enoch Arden, a rough sailor's lad
> Made orphan by a winter shipwreck, play'd
> Among the waste and lumber of the shore,
> Hard coils of cordage, swarthy fishing-nets,
> Anchors of rusty fluke, and boats updrawn;
> And built their castles of dissolving sand
> To watch them overflow'd, or following up
> And flying the white breaker, daily left
> The little footprint daily wash'd away.

Indeed the entire chain of events appears to owe much to chance, or fate. It happens fortuitously enough that 'Ten miles to northward of the narrow port/ Opened a larger haven', and as a result Enoch's economic welfare declines. He goes to sea, but 'clambering on a mast/ In harbour, by mischance he slipt and fell'. Whilst recovering he finds 'Another hand crept . . . across his trade' in a continuation of the kind of economic competition described in *Maud*. When he sets sail on the *Good Fortune*, the ship is indeed lucky at first, but 'less lucky her home-voyage'. After being, like the Ancient Mariner, becalmed, Enoch is shipwrecked upon a desert island, 'the loneliest in a lonely sea'. To some extent the island seems to mirror Enoch's own economic situation: its topography subtly repeats the geography of the fishing village at home, and serves to hint at the deadening hand of mercantile capital:

> The mountain wooded to the peak, the lawns
> And winding glades high up like ways to Heaven,
> The slender coco's drooping crown of plumes,
> The lightning flash of insect and of bird,
> The lustre of the long convolvuluses
> That coil'd around the stately stems, and ran
> Ev'n to the limit of the land,

Here Enoch reverts, like the Lotos-Eaters, to a state of nature, 'hardly human . . . Muttering and mumbling, idiotlike it seem'd', as he is perceived by his rescuers. Annie, misreading a dream in which she sees Enoch sitting beneath a palm tree, feels finally free to marry the faithful Philip. Enoch, saved by the same kind of chance which originally had led to the wreck, returns home to find another ensconced in his place, his view of the family scene through the window serving nicely to emphasize his role as archetypal outsider and victim:

> For cups and silver on the burnish'd board
> Sparkled and shone; so genial was the hearth:
> And on the right hand of the hearth he saw
> Philip, the slighted suitor of old times,
> Stout, rosy, with his babe across his knees;

Enoch turns silently away, lives a year longer as an unrecognized hermit, and dies, honoured finally by the village which has destroyed his hopes:

> So past the strong heroic soul away.
> And when they buried him the little port
> Had seldom seen a costlier funeral.

Such an act of self-abnegation, in the final movement of the poem, may be read equally as heroic self-sacrifice or suicidal neurosis. To that extent 'Enoch Arden' is a curiously open text in which the values of Victorian society are both inscribed and erased. It is clear, with hindsight, that Enoch's rescue is a mixed blessing: unlike Mariana, he would perhaps be better off to be left unvisited. This sense of equivocation marks the whole poem. When Annie turns to the Bible for guidance, for example, she places her finger at random upon the passage, 'Under the palm tree', and can uncover no meaning there. She then dreams of Enoch in heaven, and proceeds to marry on the basis of this misreading. Of Enoch's funeral, much commented upon by the poet's contemporaries, Tennyson said, 'the costly funeral is all that poor Annie could do for him after he was gone'; yet this is equally unclear in the text itself, where the temptations of what Ricks calls 'martyrdom-suicide' are explored as interestingly as they are in 'St Simeon Stylites'.

In a perceptive analysis of this somewhat maligned poem,[25] Martin Dodsworth focuses the reader's attention upon the desert island section, and seeks to defend it against the critique of the Victorian critic and political writer, Walter Bagehot. Bagehot had argued that Tennyson's description is 'absurd' because 'his hero feels nothing else but these great splendours':

We hear nothing of the physical ailments, the rough devices, the low superstitions, which really would have been the *first* things, the favourite and principal occupations of his mind.

As Dodsworth drily remarks, it's clear that Bagehot would have preferred *Robinson Crusoe*. The verbally dense, Keatsian description of the island, Dodsworth argues, is there precisely because 'Enoch *feels* nothing of the splendours described; his attention is turned completely away from them'. As the narrator remarks, 'All these he saw, but what he fain had seen/ He could not see'. The 'plenitude' of the island, that is to say, is reduced to emptiness under the blankness of Enoch's exhausted gaze. The repetitive structure of these lines seeks not only to create a gorgeous tropical glow, but also to suggest the monotony and anguish of Enoch's state:

> The blaze upon the waters to the east;
> The blaze upon his island overhead;
> The blaze upon the waters to the west;
> Then the great stars that globed themselves in Heaven,
> The hollower-bellowing ocean, and again
> The scarlet shafts of sunrise – but no sail.

*Critical Studies:* Tennyson

Dodsworth calls attention to the intransitive verbs, which reveal a sense that nothing will ever change: 'The impression left by the passage as a whole is that both Enoch and the island are emptying themselves of themselves in the process of longingly proclaiming their identities to an unregarding world.' The problem with the poem arises, in Dodsworth's reading, when Enoch returns home and retains his anonymity; the trouble here is that the poem 'wants to persuade us that very neurotic behaviour is really very good'. 'Enoch Arden' is a poem which suffers from what Dodsworth designates 'an excess of emotion' – a linguistic profusion, excess and richness which seek to cancel out the vacant loneliness of the human predicament as imaged in the tale of Enoch's plight. In the nodal scene of the outsider gazing voyeuristically at the successful rival and insider which dominates the text, Tennyson perhaps unconsciously articulates the fragmentariness of his position vis-à-vis his society. The lonely and depressed Lincolnshire outsider who achieved the laureateship seeks, in this poem, to recapture that sense of alienation and loss which had been vital to his art. If the poet is both Enoch and Philip, then 'Enoch Arden' takes on a significant emotive charge which renders it rather more than a simple exercise in the picturesque.

### 'Lucretius' (1868)

This poem takes the form of a soliloquy which voices the thoughts of Lucretius, and makes use of imagery drawn from that philosopher's *De Rerum Natura*. The poem is imagined as partly spoken by Lucretius when he is distraught with sexual dreams induced by a love philtre administered by his jealous wife. A philosopher who espouses calmness of spirit is now aroused to frenzy. The text successfully combines erotic desire, godlessness, and the sense of a mechanical universe, to produce a final scene of suicide. The first of Lucretius's dreams, for instance, is a nightmare of creation and destruction:

> . . . it seem'd
> A void was made in Nature; all her bonds
> Crack'd; and I saw the flaring atom-streams
> And torrents of her myriad universe,
> Ruining along the illimitable inane,
> Fly on to clash together again, and make
> Another and another frame of things
> For ever:

Lucretius had hoped to live virtuously, like the Epicurean gods:

Nothing to mar the sober majesties
Of settled, sweet, Epicurean life.
But now it seems some unseen monster lays
His vast and filthy hands upon my will,
Wrenching it backward into his;

Tennyson seems in this poem to be haunted by the vision of an atomistic universe such as he sometimes imagined in *In Memoriam*, and he
structures the poem as a frenzied monologue within an ironic frame.
Lucretius's speech is made up of questioning and sardonic mockery
introduced by his three dreams; although his wife appears in the framing
narrative, Lucilia and her passion do not really account for the terrifying
nature of Lucretius's frenzied visions, as in his dream of Helen:

Then, then, from utter gloom stood out the breasts,
The breasts of Helen, and hoveringly a sword
Now over and now under, now direct,
Pointed itself to pierce, but sank down shamed
At all that beauty;

Thus Lucretius's erasure of sexuality from his philosophical system
returns to haunt and destroy him in these phallic images. What mocks
and denies is the chaos underlying all human life and thought, and the
narrative moves out of control in the face of such corrosive sexuality.
Lucretius's dying response to his wife issues out of his overweening wish
to turn men into gods:

With that he drove the knife into his side:
She heard him raging, heard him fall; ran in,
Beat breast, tore hair, cried out upon herself
As having fail'd in duty to him, shriek'd
That she but meant to win him back, fell on him,
Clasp'd, kiss'd him, wail'd: he answer'd, 'Care not thou!
Thy duty? What is duty? Fare thee well!'

The search for a ground of being has in itself proved groundless.
Tennyson surely does rather more here than turn the representative of
naturalism into a 'voluptuary', as Sinfield argues. Lucretius emerges
from the text as a curiously modern figure, one whose atomism antici-
pates some aspects of nineteenth-century scientific thought, and whose
version of Epicureanism carried within it seeds of the Utilitarian philosophy. The Lucretian project has been to free men by proving that the
universe operates according to fixed laws, and by demonstrating that

there is no afterlife; but this project is undermined by the philosopher's crass underestimation of the role and pressure of the irrational in men's behaviour.

### 'The Ancient Sage' (1885)

Written after Tennyson had read the Chinese philosopher Lao-tsze, this poem presents two contradictory views. An ancient philosopher pauses beside a stream issuing from a cave to comment upon the verses of his companion, a younger man who honours him but disagrees with his philosophy of life. Those who believe that there is no power beyond nature need to delve into the cave of the self to learn that the Nameless possesses a name:

> 'For Knowledge is the swallow on the lake
> That sees and stirs the surface-shadow there
> But never yet hath dipt into the abysm,
> The Abysm of all Abysms, beneath, within
> The blue of sky and sea, the green of earth,
> And in the million-millionth of a grain
> Which cleft and cleft again for evermore,
> And ever vanishing, never vanishes,
> To me, my son, more mystic than myself,
> Or even than the Nameless is to me.'

The realm of the 'Nameless' is outside time; it is only mortals who freely divide time into such segments as 'Then' and 'When'. The sage recalls the 'passion of the past', when gleams of 'far, far away' came as boyhood intimations of immortality.

The sage concludes his message affirmatively, adjuring his auditor to 'curb the beast' within so as to 'climb the Mount of Blessing'. The argument of the poem seems to be against the undermining power of scepticism, and in favour, as Sinfield writes, of an attempt 'to push past language to a reality beyond it'. Words are 'but shadows of a shadow-world', hence the juxtaposition of the name and the Nameless, as the sage divorces his self from the symbol of that self, the name in language. Sinfield ingeniously shows how there is 'no final escape from language': as the sage returns to the 'real' world, 'I touched my limbs'. The figures of 'The Ancient Sage' are hierarchical and formal, standing stiffly with the ancient city in the background. The injunction at the close to work in 'yon dark city' is deeply pondered, and the poem strikes the reader as one of the poet's most vatic utterances.

**'Merlin and the Gleam' (1889)**

Written about the time of the poet's eightieth birthday, and set in the Isle of Wight, this poem reviews Tennyson's career in poetry: stanza two refers to the lyricism of boyhood; stanza three to the vituperations of his early critics; stanza four describes the early poems, and the following stanza characterizes the idylls; the Arthurian epic is sketched in in stanza six, and the death of Hallam and the composition of 'Morte d'Arthur' form the body of the remarkable stanza seven:

> For out of darkness
> Silent and slowly
> The Gleam, that had waned to a wintry glimmer
> On icy fallow
> And faded forest,
> Drew to the valley
> Named of the shadow,
> And slowly brightening
> Out of the glimmer,
> And slowly moving again to a melody
> Yearningly tender,
> Fell on the shadow,
> No longer a shadow,
> But clothed with The Gleam.

The quiet, stripped utterance here suggests a lifetime's immersion in poetic practice, and the verse movingly re-creates the emergence of the poetic gift after the shattering death of Hallam. Poetic inspiration, the 'Gleam' of the title, has fulfilled its promise:

> For thro' the Magic
> Of Him the Mighty,
> Who taught me in childhood,
> There on the border
> Of boundless Ocean,
> And all but in Heaven
> Hovers the Gleam.

Merlin's defeat in 'Merlin and Vivien' is the defeat of the imagination of man, but there is no defeat in this triumphant late poem. On the contrary, the old magician dies rejoicing in his creativity. The two-stress unrhymed lines, changing to four stresses under passionate feeling, enact the distillation of a full and remembered life: a renewal of language and of poetry itself is the promise of this very late and visionary work.

*Critical Studies:* Tennyson

**'Crossing the Bar' (1889)**

This is one of the finest of Tennyson's later poems, and in it the poet
looks steadily towards death. Stanzas three and four subtly repeat the
basic rhythms and syntax of the first two verses, yet with cunning vari-
ation. In each a musing exclamation is followed by a reassurance, the
long line in each case being carefully controlled and curbed by the shorter
line which follows. There have been critical objections to the appearance
of the Pilot in the final stanza; but the beauty and darkness of the waters
has been stressed, and the poem neatly produces the paradox that the
move into the boundless deep is also the turn towards the final home.
Through such imagery is a final sense of plenitude produced in the
poetry of a writer who may be termed the laureate of loss and absence.
This short and evocative poem stands, in Hallam Tennyson's phrase, as
the 'crown' of the poet's lifework, and the words 'face to face' serve to
conjure up, for the final time, the dead friend of fifty years before.
Although, as Ricks remarks in his fine reading of the poem, there are six
references to 'I' or 'me', yet 'no poem was ever less self-absorbed'. In this
final testament, Tennyson leaves the reader with a sense of the full and
tested humanity of a great poet:

> Sunset and evening star,
>    And one clear call for me!
> And may there be no moaning of the bar,
>    When I put out to sea.
>
> But such a tide as moving seems asleep,
>    Too full for sound and foam,
> When that which drew from out the boundless deep
>    Turns again home.
>
> Twilight and evre be no sadness of farewell,
>    When I embark;
>
> For tho' from out our bourne of Time and Place
>    The flood may bear me far,
> I hope to see my Pilot face to face
>    When I have crost the bar.

# Notes

1. Hopkins's letter may be read in *Gerard Manley Hopkins: Poems & Prose*, ed. W. H. Gardner (Penguin, 1981), pp. 153–7.
2. Hallam's review is reproduced in *Victorian Scrutinies*, ed. Isobel Armstrong (Athlone Press, 1972), pp. 84–101, and in an edited form in *Tennyson: The Critical Heritage*, ed. J. D. Jump (Routledge & Kegan Paul, 1967), pp. 34–49.
3. Robert Langbaum, *The Poetry of Experience* (Norton, 1963).
4. Christopher Ricks, *Tennyson* (Macmillan, 1969).
5. George Steiner, 'Privacies of Speech', in *George Steiner: A Reader* (Penguin, 1984), p. 385.
6. See Jennifer Gribble, *The Lady of Shalott in the Victorian Novel* (Macmillan, 1983).
7. Geoffrey Hartman, *Saving the Text* (Johns Hopkins University Press, 1981), pp. 110–11.
8. Alan Sinfield, *Alfred Tennyson* (Blackwell, 1986).
9. J. Killham (ed.), *Critical Essays on the Poetry of Tennyson* (Routledge & Kegan Paul, 1960), pp. 164–73.
10. Catherine Belsey, *Critical Practice* (Methuen, 1980), p. 132.
11. P. Rabinow (ed.), *The Foucault Reader* (Penguin, 1986), pp. 300ff.
12. Steiner, *op. cit.*, p. 313.
13. Reprinted in J. Killham, *op. cit.*, pp. 177–85.
14. *Ibid.*, pp. 192–203.
15. Gillian Beer, *Darwin's Plots* (Ark, 1985), p. 127.
16. Sinfield, *op. cit.*, pp. 127–52.
17. Jeffrey Weeks, *Sex, Politics & Society* (Longman, 1981), p. 109.
18. In *Post-Structuralist Readings of English Poetry*, ed. R. Machin & C. Norris (Cambridge University Press, 1987), pp. 308–31.
19. In *Untying the Text*, ed. R. Young (Routledge & Kegan Paul, 1981), pp. 207–22.
20. '"What is it, that has been done?": the central problem of *Maud*', *Essays in Criticism*, 24 (1974), pp. 356–62.
21. 'Tennyson's *Maud*: the function of the imagery', in Killham, *op. cit.*, pp. 219–35.
22. See, in addition to Killham, *op. cit.*, Philip Drew, 'Tennyson and the dramatic monologue', in *Tennyson*, ed. D. J. Palmer (Bell, 1973), pp. 115–46.
23. 'What is an Author?' in Rabinow, *op. cit.*, pp. 102–3.
24. See P. G. Scott, *Tennyson's Enoch Arden: A Victorian Best Seller* (The Tennyson Society, 1970).
25. 'Patterns of morbidity: repetition in Tennyson's poetry', in *The Major Victorian Poets: A Reconstruction*, ed. I. Armstrong (Routledge & Kegan Paul, 1969), pp. 7–34.

# Select Bibliography

1. *Editions*
   *The Poems of Tennyson*, ed. C. Ricks (Longman, 1969)
   *The Poems of Tennyson*, ed. C. Ricks (revised edn, 3 vols.) (Longman, 1987)

2. *Biography*
   Martin, R. B. *Tennyson: The Unquiet Heart* (Clarendon Press, 1980)
   Tennyson, C. & Dyson, H. *The Tennysons* (Macmillan, 1974)

3. *Critical Studies*
   Armstrong, Isobel (ed.) *Victorian Scrutinies* (Athlone Press, 1972)
   Culler, Dwight *The Poetry of Tennyson* (Yale University Press, 1977)
   Gransden, K. W. *Tennyson: In Memoriam* (Edward Arnold, 1964)
   Hunt, J. D. (ed.) *In Memoriam: Casebook* (Macmillan, 1970)
   Jump, J. D. (ed.) *Tennyson: The Critical Heritage* (Routledge & Keegan Paul, 1967)
   Killham, John (ed.) *Critical Essays on the Poetry of Tennyson* (Routledge & Keegan Paul, 1960)
   Palmer, D. J. (ed.) *Tennyson* (Bell, 1973)
   Pinion, F. B. *A Tennyson Companion* (Macmillan, 1984)
   Pitt, Valerie *Tennyson Laureate* (Barrie & Rockliff, 1962)
   Ricks, Christopher *Tennyson* (Macmillan, 1972)
   Sinfield, Alan *Alfred Tennyson* (Blackwell, 1986)
   Thomson, Alistair *The Poetry of Tennyson* (Routledge & Keegan Paul, 1986)

# FOR THE BEST IN PAPERBACKS, LOOK FOR THE

In every corner of the world, on every subject under the sun, Penguin represents quality and variety – the very best in publishing today.

For complete information about books available from Penguin – including Pelicans, Puffins, Peregrines and Penguin Classics – and how to order them, write to us at the appropriate address below. Please note that for copyright reasons the selection of books varies from country to country.

**In the United Kingdom:** For a complete list of books available from Penguin in the U.K., please write to *Dept E.P., Penguin Books Ltd, Harmondsworth, Middlesex, UB7 0DA*

**In the United States:** For a complete list of books available from Penguin in the U.S., please write to *Dept BA, Penguin, 299 Murray Hill Parkway, East Rutherford, New Jersey 07073*

**In Canada:** For a complete list of books available from Penguin in Canada, please write to *Penguin Books Canada Ltd, 2801 John Street, Markham, Ontario L3R 1B4*

**In Australia:** For a complete list of books available from Penguin in Australia, please write to the *Marketing Department, Penguin Books Australia Ltd, P.O. Box 257, Ringwood, Victoria 3134*

**In New Zealand:** For a complete list of books available from Penguin in New Zealand, please write to the *Marketing Department, Penguin Books (NZ) Ltd, Private Bag, Takapuna, Auckland 9*

**In India:** For a complete list of books available from Penguin, please write to *Penguin Overseas Ltd, 706 Eros Apartments, 56 Nehru Place, New Delhi, 110019*

**In Holland:** For a complete list of books available from Penguin in Holland, please write to *Penguin Books Nederland B.V., Postbus 195, NL–1380AD Weesp, Netherlands*

**In Germany:** For a complete list of books available from Penguin, please write to *Penguin Books Ltd, Friedrichstrasse 10 – 12, D–6000 Frankfurt Main 1, Federal Republic of Germany*

**In Spain:** For a complete list of books available from Penguin in Spain, please write to *Longman Penguin España, Calle San Nicolas 15, E–28013 Madrid, Spain*

# FOR THE BEST IN PAPERBACKS, LOOK FOR THE 🐧

## PENGUIN MASTERSTUDIES AND CRITICAL STUDIES

This comprehensive list, designed for advanced level and first-year under-graduate studies, includes:

**SUBJECTS**
Applied Mathematics
Biology
Drama: Text into Performance
Geography
Pure Mathematics

**LITERATURE**
Absalom and Achitophel
Barchester Towers
Dr Faustus
Eugénie Grandet
The Great Gatsby
Gulliver's Travels
Joseph Andrews
The Mill on the Floss
A Passage to India
Persuasion *and* Emma
Portrait of a Lady
Tender Is the Night
Vanity Fair
The Waste Land

**CHAUCER**
The Knight's Tale
The Miller's Tale
The Nun's Priest's Tale
The Pardoner's Tale
The Prologue to The Canterbury
    Tales
A Chaucer Handbook

**SHAKESPEARE**
Antony & Cleopatra
Hamlet
King Lear
Measure for Measure
Much Ado About Nothing
Othello
The Tempest
A Shakespeare Handbook